The Elusive Gift of Tragedy

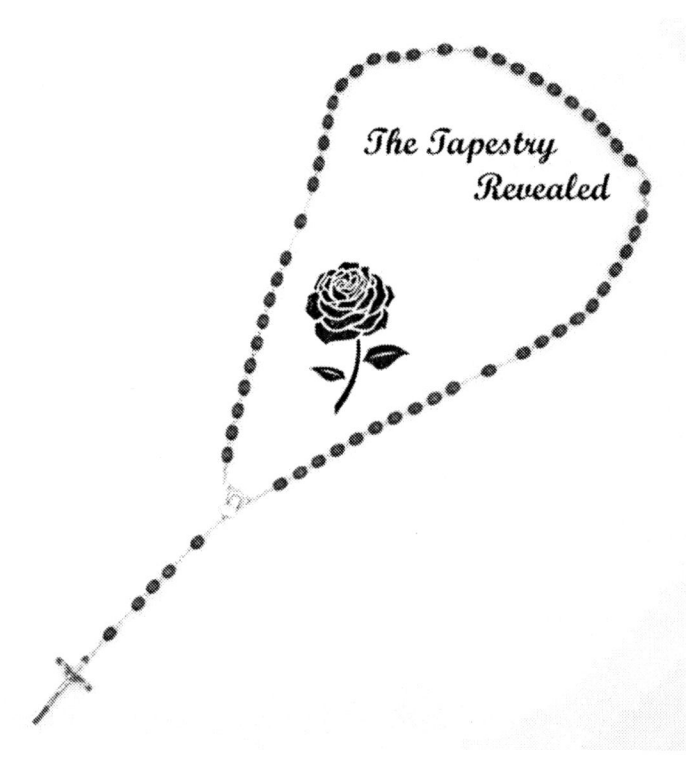

What Others Are Saying About This Book

"A labor of love for mothers who need answers."

— Beverly Bishop, RN, BSW, M.Ed.

"This book will open doorways of understanding and refreshing hope for people experiencing the depth of pain of the loss of a child. The author's piercing honesty and drive to know pulls the reader along with astonishing detail. And her friendly style is easy to read while emotionally revealing.

"The book allows the reader to glimpse soul's viewpoint of the multi-faceted experience of motherhood, love and loss. It is so important that people come to realize children are independent souls with their own agendas and that parents being parents must start remembering that they too are souls with agendas, different from their parents and their own children.

"This book will help readers pick up this thread of consciousness, so they can begin to accept and release their attachments to how society and culture program us into believing life should be. We need to stop the myth and start to accept the powerful souls we really are, honor our choices and the choices of others regardless of what we desire. And in so doing, recognize we cannot ever be separated from anyone – not those we love or those we hate. But rather, as we master the truth of our very essence, we come into a peaceful neutral zone, a place of perfection without hate or attachment or the physical emotional love, but rather into the power of love – the gift of unity with all creation and its Creator."

—— Michele Avanti CAP, EFT-3

The Elusive Gift of Tragedy

Regina Murphy

Love in Action Press

The Elusive Gift of Tragedy
By Regina Rose Murphy

Published by:
Love in Action Press
Las Vegas, Nevada

www.LoveInActionInc.com

Copyright © 2007 Regina Murphy All Rights Reserved
ISBN-13: 978-0-9800365-2-7

Contents of this book are copyrighted. No part may be reproduced or introduced into a retrieval system, or transmitted, in any form or by any means (electronic, mechanical, photocopying, recording or otherwise) without written permission of the publisher or author, except for brief quotations by reviewers and other brief instances where full credit of source is stated. The author and publisher of this book do not dispense medical advice or prescribe any technique as a form of treatment for physical conditions or problems and therefore assume no responsibility for your actions. The techniques, ideas, and suggestions in this book are not intended as a substitute for medical advice.

All photographs referred to in this book may be viewed on www.LoveInActionInc.com by clicking on "Book Photo Gallery."

Interior and Cover Design by Tony Stubbs, www.tjpublish.com

Printed in the United States

Table of Contents

Section One: The Threads That Bind Our Tender Souls 1
1. The Other Side of the Tapestry 3
2. John Jr. Enters into Separation 13
3. The Divorce – The First Cut Is the Deepest 17
4. Key Players are Woven into the Tapestry 21
5. Adolescence Arrives in All Its Glory 23
6. September 11, 2001, New York 31
7. My Purpose Becomes Clear 39
8. More Lessons for John 47
9. 2004: We Discover the Healing Power of Sound ... 55
10. Nine Months Remain - A Reverse Pregnancy 63
11. So Much to Be Experienced in So Little Time 69
12. The Blessed Mother Prepares Me 83
13. The Final Touches of a Life 93

Section Two: Focal Point of the Tapestry 101
14. A New Form Is Taken 103
15. The Shock Is Over; the Grief Begins 125
16. Communications Across the Veil 133
17. Grief Grows Like a Weeping Willow 145
18. Death Knocks Again 151
19. My Camera Pierces the Veil 159
20. Pre-Birth Planning 169
21. My Gift From John - The Pink Ball of Light 187
22. The Revelations of the Tapestry 193

Afterword
- Statistics 2004: Death by Overdose 204
- References 205
- End Note 208

Appendices:
A. Mother Mary Channel 209
B. Thought Field Therapy 217
C. Emotional Freedom Techniques (EFT) 219
D. Emotional Sound Technique (EST) 221
E. The AIM Program 223
F. The Tragic Consequences of Drugging Our Children 224
G. Photo Gallery 227

IN MEMORY OF MY SON, JOHN

ENTERED the HUMAN FORM of SEPARATION
FEBRUARY 20TH 1986

BORN AGAIN INTO A HIGHER VIBRATION OF
UNCONDITIONAL LOVE
OCTOBER 2, 2005

The pink ball of light on the front cover is an actual photo taken by Regina. Ultimately, she learned that it is her son, John, in his energy form.

Dedication

Dedicated to all parents who search in desperation to help ease the emotional and physical pain of our children

Special Thanks

In July 2005, I heard my editor, Tony Stubbs, speak on the monthly Lightworker Virtual Light broadcast about how to write a book. I knew at that moment the message of "using sound on the EFT points" needed to be taught and be available to the general public. Tony planted a seed in me, although I didn't know he would be present throughout the process of John's death each time I couldn't continue to write, he would say just the right thing with his gentle English wisdom that would help me out of a very stuck place. I know now that this book was to heal me and that as a practitioner in the healing arts, I'm sure the process is the best energy medicine I could have incorporated into my journey. I would advise everyone who has something to say to write a book. Even if no one but you ever reads it, you have given yourself a grand gift. To Tony, I can only say, "Thank you for the role you have chosen to play as the 'Great healer' through words that you are."

From my personal experience, watching a child suffer is the most difficult of all human challenges and that is the obvious risk when giving birth. David and I wanted a child together but were past our childbearing years when we met. This book has been like giving birth together. We have enjoyed the birth process of this book more than anything else we have shared. We now begin the process of raising this child and are looking forward to that journey. During the writing process, every time I wanted to go to a movie, David would say, "We have to get this book done, hon." Every time I told him I'd decided not to finish the book, he didn't reply, but just waited until my internal struggle ended and we just kept going. Every morning before he got out of bed, David asked, "Do you have anything for me to read?" And he spent two hours correcting for every hour I spent writing.

I am so blessed to be among the few to know what it is like to be loved and supported with unconditional love from a life partner while in human form. I wish this for all of humanity. David allows me to experience heaven on earth, a place of love. Thank you, darling!

Finally, I must thank the hundreds of loving hands that have reached out to support me through my life, especially my physical and spiritual family.

Foreword by Tony Stubbs

In *The Elusive Gift of Tragedy*, author Regina Murphy provides parents with an impressive arsenal of tools to guide their children through today's perilous minefield of childhood to healthy, productive adulthood. First, she and her son, John, experienced years of consequences resulting from a primitive treatment her son experienced at birth, a practice now thankfully abandoned. Regina discovers tangible tools and incredible modalities that allow us to remove negative energy and remap the subconscious mind.

Next the book explores the pre-existence of the soul and the beauty of pre-life planning. Then we learn that John's soul has a huge mission that spans many lifetimes – the search for, and the expression of, the purity of unconditional love. His failure to isolate that purity in his most recent lifetime opened him up to the frustration and the self-destructive behaviors prevalent in today's teenagers. Add to that society's demand for instant gratification and a materialistic mentality, and we have a perfect storm of cultural disintegration.

Having set up lives rich in "unexploded bombs," Regina and John explore the new tools to defuse them. The first is Regina's enduring faith in a Higher Power, manifesting as angels and Mother Mary, the Mother of all mothers – a faith John acknowledges as his rock.

Regina then leads into a new modality of her own – Emotional Sound Technique- that involves the use of tuning forks placed on a specific quartz crystal applied directly to key emotionally related meridian points on the body. To be honest, this therapy is not new; we used it long ago in many ancient cultures. And to top it all, Regina has discovered that she can photograph the life force energy changes when using these modalities as well as many dimensions of reality in every camera she owns. This book provides pointers to resources by which you can become an expert practitioner for yourself and your kids ... and who knows, maybe even save their lives.

Will some readers find this book a stretch? Undoubtedly, but as Albert Einstein said, "No problem can be solved at the same level at which it was created." Today's parents are faced with momentous challenges regarding their children. In order to meet these challenges, parents must transcend them, and *The Elusive Gift of Tragedy* provides a wide range of tools to do just that.

Oh, and the final gift? Proof of survival of death. This book implodes the concept of death as the cessation of being. In its pages we meet John, still the same vibrant, dynamic being he was in a physical body, only now he has the wisdom of Solomon and absolute dedication to the welfare of today's youth.

Together Regina and John are an unstoppable force who will take you to places you never knew existed. Just have an open mind and the courage to journey with them for the rewards are beyond your imagining.

After all, aren't your kids worth it?

> — Tony Stubbs, author of *An Ascension Handbook, Living With Soul, It's All About Control* and *Death Without Fear*

Introduction

In September of 2001, I made an appointment with Doctor Fuller Royal of The Nevada Clinic that saved my life. I had been bleeding for almost a year and my gynecologist, although very competent, could do nothing to help. Even strong doses of progesterone did nothing. Being a massage therapist at the St. Therese Center, I thought the oils I used or the transdermal medications from the AIDS patients I massaged were getting into my system and affecting my hormones.. The critical point came three days before 9/11 when I spent the night at the Marriott World Trade Center and hemorrhaged through the night. Upon returning to Las Vegas, I went to see Dr. Fuller Royal and all he did was tap on certain meridian points and sent me home. To my shock and amazement, the bleeding stopped and I made a full recovery. I had no idea until years later why or how this worked, or the full impact that session would have on my life.

Being lucky enough to have an aura camera and being able to devote all of my time to Energy Medicine and research, I studied and experimented continually in this and related fields. My son, John, who had extreme emotional problems due to birth trauma was the reason I worked so hard to find answers to help people feel better without chemicals. The results I had with him and all my clients were amazing. Later, I added sound to the modalities and now a specific use of crystals that clarifies and amplifies the sound on the meridian points.

My son died of an accidental prescription drug overdose in 2005 and I used these tools to help me function. Shortly after that, a rare gift I believe came from my son allowed me to photograph the subtle energies in my healing room. My ordinary digital camera began to show what was happening in the energetic field during a session. Spirits, angels, energy and emotions of many different dimensions began appearing in the photos. Each time I bought a new camera, the same thing happened. This gift of being able to actually see energy opened the other side of the veil for me and quickly guided me to some of the most basic and effective forms of healing available to all of us, and the power behind them. Since the basics of Energy Medicine and Energy Psychology are like trying to describe color to a person born without sight, this book is like a parable about healing told through the story of the life and death of my son rather than a scientific approach. Those books and "how to" websites are all in the appendix, as well as a companion DVD. Tuning forks and crystal sets are available through my website. The story behind these discoveries and the lessons learned along the way is what makes it come alive.

With Love
Regina

Section One

The Threads That Bind Our Tender Souls

You could look at life planning as a huge tapestry, one that would cover the wall of a room and much, much more, and each thread is an option within that plan. There are literally billions of threads within each tapestry of life, and each is an option. And although we may plan a specific tapestry when coming in, it is almost guaranteed that, in the physical, the tapestry will be shifted due to our free will. It is one of the reasons we leave ourselves so many options and so many connections.

Chapter One

The Other Side of the Tapestry

The Joy

The timeline of lessons and what I have learned as John's mother is as accurate as I can recall. It was pointed out to me in the early stages of writing the book that I had forgotten the Joy. For this I must thank my niece Jen.

Each day of our lives as a family was sprinkled with joy, just like fairy dust. The financial gift of owning J & R Flooring allowed us the money, the connections and the resources to travel and shower our children with great gifts, lessons in hard work, respect for every one who worked for us, and gratitude for those we were privileged to serve. These lessons were not taught; they were caught. My daughters continue to bless the flooring industry with love and feminine leadership. I am very, very proud of them. When David, now my husband, came into my life, he continued to gift our family with joy every step of the way. John's life was filled with music, laughter, vacations, toys and a huge family who adored him. He became the party planner, the travel agent and the resource for creative musicians and wrote music that will live on forever. He was the guy in the neighborhood who everybody loved. He didn't fit into our current model of learning but he educated himself through the Science and Discovery TV channels and his very favorite, Animal Planet. I was relieved he had already crossed over before the death of Steve Irwin (aka the Crocodile Hunter) because he would have been inconsolable after Steve's tragic death. As it turned out, John may have been first in line to welcome Steve to the other side.

John was always quick to point out to his friends and me when we were being cruel or judgmental of someone or something. Once, I made an ignorant snotty comment about the religion of Rastafari, and John insisted that I watch a documentary on Bob Marley. As we watched it together, he pointed out how much Bob Marley's music contributed to create peace in his homeland. Not one day of John's life went by that he didn't have joy as an ingredient. He watched as our family business always took care of those in need, and as people in crisis came through our front door at any hour of the day or night.

Compassion and service took no holidays in our family. John worked at the St. Therese Center for HIV, even when people were still afraid of the word AIDS. These lessons helped him become who he was. He was equally at home having lunch with casino owners as chatting with the guy who lived in his car parked in the company parking lot; both were important to him. His birthdays, summer vacations, road trips, weekend campouts, poker parties and chess games were legendary. His bedroom music studio was a focal point for the creativity of an entire neighborhood to blossom and grow. His website and Myspace page are filled with memories of joy, and on a daily basis, he continues to communicate and help from the other side of the veil.

Last but not least, each time he got into an argument with his father, he knew it was because his father wanted only the best for him. Every criticism contained the hope that John would be happy and successful in life ... and he knew it. He also knew he had a musical gift his father admired, and that admiration was actually all he ever wanted, except for his yearning that we humans could all learn to love one another. From the first day of his life, John was my teacher, and all his hardships only served to help and bless humanity. The ripple of his life teaches us we are all connected, and we each hold an important piece of God's plan ... if only we can learn to see beyond the veil of illusion.

There Is No Book on the Shelf

Today's turbulent sea, in which our children must grow up, is full of self-doubt and the need for acceptance by family and peers. It offers "legal" and "illegal" drugs as answers to the myriad of challenges they must overcome in order to become adults. Many of them will drown in the ocean of drugs that today are so freely available on the streets and the Internet, and many will never reach the shores of adulthood.

My only wish is that one parent is able to use what I have learned to more clearly see that their children's emotional pain and hurting can be lessened and their destructive behavior can be changed at an early age. If this occurs, I have done my job.

I watched my son agonize about how he learned and behaved. I studied and read as much as I could about behavioral problems and learning disabilities. I began learning about and became certified in applying simple Energy Medicine techniques that greatly changed John's behavior. He developed an interest in music and started to change some of his values. It was a relief to see that changes were possible for John. I hope to introduce parents to these techniques to help reduce the emotional trauma which children and parents can feel when they seem to have no answers. This book will give you real answers that are not found in any book on the shelf. It is an account of what parents can do for their children at little or no cost. Mothers spend nine months developing the bodies of their children for birth. I'm asking you to spend a couple of hours learning how to help them process their emotions. In this book, you will learn of positive documented results and changes that can occur in their behavioral patters.

The Backdrop of My Life

"Born the fourth of six Murphy girls in Brooklyn, New York" in 1953 paints a picture so I'll skip the boring details. The most exciting thing about my life as a child was trying to stay out of trouble at St. Michael's Catholic school and trying to decide which convent I was going to join as soon as they would take me. I took religion very seriously and was sure being a nun would make me happy for life.

The movie, *The Song of Bernadette*, changed my life in that my faith in God and Mother Mary really took hold. In second grade, I played an angel in The Story of Fatima, which reinforced my belief in the unseen. (I did not yet have a grasp on the fact that I was a born rule-breaker. I was born on the same day as Tony Spilotro, the notorious Las Vegas mob figure, so if there is any truth to Natal Astrology, you know I would not have made a good nun.)

Living in a predominantly Irish neighborhood, I naturally fell in love with an Italian boy, "John the butcher's son," as my mother called him. He lived a few miles from us and delivered meat for his father, who owned a local butcher shop. When John and I got engaged, I asked him, "Why are you marrying me?" fully expecting a romantic answer. He seriously said, "For the wedding gifts." I thought that was a joke. It wasn't. He meant it.

I wanted to go to college but my mother discouraged me for two reasons. First she said, "Marriages never work out if only the girl is educated," and second, "The sooner you're working, the sooner you can pay rent." These seemed like valid points and I was never thrilled about school anyway.

We weren't married a year before we left Brooklyn for Las Vegas, or "Sin City." No one believed we were serious and thought we would be back in a week, but soon half of Brooklyn had followed us out to Las Vegas.

John had some experience in the carpeting field so we opened our own small business – J & R Flooring in 1978. Vegas was still a small town then but growing fast. You didn't need to be the sharpest knife in the drawer to do well in a city rapidly building new hotels and casinos, all of which needed lots of carpet.

I gave birth to two beautiful girls: Jamie in 1976 and Michelle in 1981. Carpet became our life and still is for our children. In 1982, things started to get a little bumpy. The business grew, the family grew and all the natural challenges of life in the fast lane served to provide a never ending saga of drama and excitement. My husband, John Sr., almost died on my second daughter's first birthday. One year later, both my parents died, soon to be followed by my niece Jen contracting cancer and my sister Ann having a stroke. My son, John, was born in 1986 and my husband asked me for a divorce in 1993. Three years later, I retired from J & R Flooring and began my path as a therapist in the healing arts.

My life's rocky experiences all served me well as preparation for the field of healing. I believe healing actually occurs everywhere you are and has nothing to do with medicine or hospitals.

My first clients were the thousands of carpet installers who we employed; only none of us knew it back then. Of course, my greatest teacher was my son, who daily continues to teach me and push me past my comfort zone from the other side of the veil.

John Sr. Close Call

Four years prior to John's birth, my husband, John Sr., and I were still in what I thought to be the perfect family. We had two girls, Jamie age five and Michelle, almost one year old. We were on our way to Disneyland for a vacation after having worked all weekend at a church bazaar selling carpet remnants in the parish flea market. John Sr. had eaten clams at the bazaar and was feeling queasy as we began the trip. By the time we reached California, we were headed to the hospital ER and that began the journey of a ruptured appendix and shock lung. On the seventh night in the hospital, the doctors said it was highly unlikely John Sr. would survive the night. I could not believe what was happening. I was alone in the hospital and it was about nine o'clock. John's mother was with me in California but was asleep in the hotel. I could see the nurses putting John on a bed of ice. One of the nurses told me I would not be allowed into the room until I was completely calm. I called John Sr.'s father and told him to come to California. I called everyone I knew and begged them to pray that John Sr. would not die. I had my parents organize a Rosary at my home and asked everyone to pray all night long. I wanted heaven to know I could not accept this death sentence. I became more upset with each phone call I made. One of the nurses came in to see if I was OK but saw that I was getting further and further away from "being calm." She lovingly put her arm around me and said, "You need to call someone who can calm you down."

My mentor and business partner in the building we occupied, Paul Faulkner, always had a way of calming me down. He was a general contractor and J & R Flooring did all of the flooring installation contracts for his accounts. As a young small business owner in Vegas, everything was always a crisis in my eyes and Paul would put things in perspective for me. Meeting payroll, keeping the hotel owners happy and paying our suppliers was a huge burden which caused me to be under constant pressure. Years later I found out that this one phone call to Paul changed my entire future, because it saved my husband's life that night and ultimately allowed my son to be born and fulfill his destiny. After I called Paul and he calmed me down so I could spend the night at my husband's side, he made a phone call to his very close friend. He was the chief-of-staff at the prestigious Scripps Clinic. This is the first of many significant and life-altering interweaving between my family and the Faulkner family that would span generations.

Within a few hours, the head of Infectious Disease from Scripps Clinic took charge of John's Sr.'s case. He met with me but gave little hope for John Sr.'s survival. John's mother took a cab to the hospital and stayed with me through the long and treacherous night. John Sr.'s mother and I took turns for naps in the next room so he would never be left alone. We were exhausted from the days leading up to this, and watching John Sr. fight for his life was almost unbearable. If they had kept him completely sedated, he would have died so he was always awake and aware he was fighting for his life. I would show him pictures of our children and literally beg him to hang on. Each breath he took required all of his strength. The critical care coordinator even told me to begin looking into transporting his body back to Las Vegas based on his current condition. I was still in my twenties and simply could not conceive that my husband could die. He was the love of my life, my best friend, my partner, the father of my children ... and I adored him. Finally, the doctor suggested putting him on a respirator, and told me, "Most likely he'll never come off it again. If we do not put him on the respirator, he would certainly die. On life support, he could live a very long time as a vegetable."

As next-of-kin, I had to make this decision alone, and I chose to keep him alive at all costs. Later that night, when they took him to the operating room to insert the respirator, I told his mother, "I know he'll live because I know someday, I'll have a son named John." For six days and nights, his life hung by a fine thread.

Watching my husband struggle for his life was highly stressful. When they finally got him off the respirator, I couldn't wait for his first words. I remember I had promised him anything if he got well. Knowing he was materialistic, I mentioned many things as bribes to keep him fighting. I also knew that when people almost die, they have religious experiences that completely change their outlook on life, often making them very spiritual. I was also told that his vocal cords might be very damaged so there were many things crossing my mind. After what seemed like endless delays, they got him off the respirator and I waited anxiously to hear what he had to say. He struggled with two words – "Touring Coup." After about the third time, I asked, "What are you talking about?"

He said, "That's the kind of Cadillac I want."

This was truly a sign of things to come. He did NOT have a religious experience, as a matter of fact; "things" became way more important to him from that moment on.

I still harbored the overwhelming certainty that he would live and father a son. After five turbulent weeks, he recovered enough to leave the hospital but was never the same. It was as though he was angry at still being alive. His whole outlook on life was different; he was always filled with anger and fought with me continuously. I believed it was him who had changed but it could have been me.

The next three years brought nothing but intense hardship. My father confided in me that during the rosary that night, both of my parents asked God to take them instead of John Sr.. Within six months, even though they were both only sixty and in relatively good health, my mother passed away. Six months later my father died. Two years later my niece Jen, eleven at the time, was diagnosed with a very rare form of lymphoma and she spent six months at Sloan Kettering Hospital undergoing cancer treatments and grueling chemotherapy. I had promised her that when she got out of Sloan Kettering Hospital, I would come back for a week and we would do anything she wanted. That day arrived and as I prepared for the trip my husband told me, "If you go to New York, you'll find divorce papers on your desk when you return." He was looking for a way out of this marriage.

I cried, but told him I had to go, and he knew I could not break this promise. We made love for what I believed would be the last time because I didn't think he'd change his mind about the divorce if I went to visit Jen. I went to New York anyway and a few weeks after my return I realized that I was pregnant. This revelation was very upsetting to my husband because he now felt totally trapped. I, however, was happy because I knew I'd have my son.

Chapter Two

John Jr. Enters into Separation

The pregnancy and birth were brutal on me and his father's resentment of me grew stronger by the day. When John was born via C-section, his liver function was a problem. He was taken away from me at birth and put into an incubator, tied down so a sun lamp would cover all his body and he was blindfolded to protect his eyes. He was kept in this inhumane position for twelve days. No eye contact, limited touch. When I tried to nurse him, he wouldn't eat so the nurses fed him formula in my absence. (As the research about the importance of touch and eye contact became more mainstream, such brutal procedures were phased out.)

I had been released from the hospital three days after the C-section and had to drive myself back and forth to the hospital several times a day to try to feed him. In addition to John Sr.'s anger and the effects of his severe Tourette Syndrome,[1] I was suffering from exhaustion, fatigue and depression, and am

---

1 A neurological disorder presenting in childhood, characterized by physical and speech tics that ebb and flow in severity.

sure our son absorbed all those emotions from us.[2] We had a real rough start and baby John was getting hit from every direction—genetics, birth trauma, a depressed mother, and a father who, I thought, wished his son didn't exist. How much more damage could a newborn have taken?

Once we all recovered from this traumatic birth experience, we resumed life as a happy family, or at least we pretended to be a happy family. I especially was pretty good at convincing myself everything was fine.

In John's early years, he was much loved and nurtured, and his sisters and grandparents were always there for him, as were both of his parents. He was so cute it was hard not to spoil him. By the time he was four, he started showing signs of being a little too spoiled. Also, I realized there was something very different about him compared with his sisters. One of the things that stuck out in my mind was that he was exceptionally uncontrollable on trips. The relevance of this to his birth trauma was discovered only after I did research after his death. I knew Tourette Syndrome symptoms start to show up around the age of four and this condition is mostly passed down from father to son, so my focus was on that, and only that.

At that time, I believed the only answer for these behavioral problems was prescription drugs such as Ritalin, Catapress and Zoloft. The best doctors in the field of medical genetics were treating him, and by the time he was six, he was on at least three medications. My life revolved around little John's behavior, and I became a recluse because I hated taking him anywhere in public due to his inability to control himself. He would have temper tantrums in public and throw himself on the floor.

---

2   Bruce Lipton, a cell biologist, discusses this in great detail in his book *The Biology of Belief*.

John Sr. had a spending addiction and went to the mall every night, taking the girls with him, which gave me quality alone time with John. I soon realized John was going to have emotional problems that would be difficult to deal with in later life.

After one or two more years of John Sr.'s "ten-day golf trips" every month, it became evident to everyone except me that the marriage was over. I considered myself a "Good Catholic" and truly believed in the "Til death do us part" thing, so the thought of divorce never entered my mind.

Chapter Three

The Divorce – The First Cut Is the Deepest

May 1993 hit me like a nightmare I would never wake up from. Because I kept so incredibly busy, I was emotionally unavailable for anyone. Between running J & R Flooring, raising the three children and taking care of everyone in need who crossed my path, and my "need to be needed" syndrome, I was blinded by the pace and the fury of my life. Keeping busy was my way of staying in denial that my marriage was over. As it turned out, I was the "bug that hit the windshield." Being the drama queen and eternal martyr, I moved out of our home, "The Del Rey House" as we still call it, only days after John Sr. told me he wanted a divorce. He, of course, didn't try to stop me from leaving. A couple of weeks later, I opened the cellular phone bill and was blindsided by the next shock. There were numerous calls to my friend, the designer for our largest client. Upon confronting John Sr., he admitted that she was to be his next wife. The stress of waiting for the final divorce decree and still working at J & R Flooring with my ex-to-be and his wife-to-be took me from a "little crazy" to a "raving lunatic."

At a tender age of seven, the divorce was more than our son John's little heart could bear. Many children have no dads or lose them in war or divorce, but this was exceptionally traumatic. Since his father's new wife and her son had been close friends of ours, and suddenly little John's dad belonged to his friend, this was inconceivable to him. Now his friend, the new stepbrother who was better in school and always behaved, became the favorite child of John Sr., if not in reality, for sure in John's mind. This was to be the constant thorn in my son's heart.

The Bar

To top it all off, I made the worst possible choice anyone in my position could ever make. At a time when I should have been focusing all my attention on my children, I ignored their needs and bought a bar… a decision that added much more stress on the children. Again I was using a distraction to avoid facing reality. No matter how hard everyone tried to talk me out of buying it, I did not listen. I was the proverbial train heading for a wreck and there was no force on earth powerful enough to stop me. To this day, I cannot figure out what I was thinking. I've hated bars ever since I was a child. I think I rationalized buying the bar with, "I can listen to everybody's problems and make money at the same time."

It doesn't take a genius to figure out this wouldn't work out for me. Buying a bar in Nevada is like a prison sentence that takes an Act of Congress to get out of. Three minutes after signing the papers, I realized I'd made the biggest mistake of my life and it took three years of $14,000 a month in losses to get rid of the bar. (When I cross over, the most pressing question I'll ask my guides and teachers will be: "Why did I buy that bar?" I'm still holding some glimmer of hope that some good will come from those years that I haven't yet figured out. So far, the best I've come up with is: "If you haven't been through hell, you won't recognize heaven when you get there.")

For John, the years I owned the bar were difficult. By second grade, he couldn't keep up in school. His test scores showed he was at 99% in problem solving and below 50% in almost every other area. Worst of all, it was impossible to read anything he wrote. Homework was not going to be on my "things to do" list and I decided to let John and his teachers deal with it. Although I did enroll him in Sylvan and paid for all sorts of tutors, I knew I was not going to spend my life yelling at him every night to do better. So, every night when he told me he had finished his homework, I pretended to believe him. He knew he was looked down upon because he couldn't write and this seriously affected his self-esteem.

By third grade, his poor grades caught up with him and he felt so terrible about himself that he would have "accidents" in his pants at school. It wasn't bad enough that he felt stupid and fat but now everyone, including me, yelled at him in the car if he had an "accident."

It never occurred to me at the time that his being over weight also added additional stress. Over weight children are often forced to sit in a "one size fits all" desk that is too small for them. This is especially true for children with anxiety disorders. This confinement is additional stress on these children.

John's doctors had him on so many medications for his behavioral problems that I eventually came to question whether those medications were actually causing his problems.[1] I took him to a kinesiologist who used muscle testing and he told me, "John is in renal failure due to the Zoloft, so I'm taking him

---

[1] See Appendix F for an excellent article by Dr. Joseph Mercola titled *The Tragic Consequences of Drugging Our Children* and a shocking one-hour documentary by Gary Null titled *The Drugging of Our Children*.

off Zoloft." Magically, the "accident" problem seemed to go away shortly after that.

Shame and humiliation were John's constant companions, which led to a true sense of failure and self-hatred before his ninth birthday. He wanted only to be treated with respect but it wasn't happening, which caused his emotions to spiral completely out of control. Throughout all of this, I could see his giant heart filled with a sadness that would break your heart ... unless you happened to be John Sr. Only disappointment showed in his dad's eyes, which John felt deeply I know.

I spoiled him in every way I could because I couldn't fix the problem. I remember taking him to see the movie, Mrs. Doubtfire, the first Thanksgiving after the divorce. He came home and broke the kitchen chairs because he was so upset. This movie portrayed a recently divorced father, played by Robin Williams, who went to extremes to spend time with his children, even dressing up as a housekeeper/nanny. He watched that movie over and over wishing things were different for him. I would strive not to cry in front of him when we watched it together. He was so sensitive that even as a little boy he hated to see anyone get upset or cry. As if all of this wasn't bad enough on his emotions, I married the manager of my bar. The marriage lasted only for 100 days, but it just added to John's insecurities and our instability. Our life was not a sitcom like Cheers, for laughter was simply not a part of it.

Chapter Four

Key Players Are Woven into the Tapestry

Finally, for the first time in almost three years, something good for John was about to happen. We often visited my sister and John had made friends with some kids in the neighborhood. A house became available for rent near my sister's house, so he would be very close to all his new friends. The prospect of us moving into that house made him so happy that I was determined to do anything I could to make it happen. His friends really loved him and, with them, he was able to regain a little self-esteem. These new friends were easy to love back, and we all watched out for each other's children. His depression lifted a little and there was some light at the end of the tunnel. He made another friend, Jack, who was overweight just like John, and that helped him with that issue. He now had a friend with the same problem. We took Jack on trips with us and, all in all, he had a little break from depression as a little joy came into his life. Jack would remain John's best friend right up until the end.

With the arrival of my first grandchild and my getting rid of the bar, things were going pretty well for John and me. I had finished massage school and was running a small residential offshoot of J & R Flooring. John was starting junior high.

My Beloved David Enters the Picture

At the end of summer 1997, I reacquainted myself with David Coffey, a CPA, I had known years earlier. We had first met when we were both on the board of the Tourette Syndrome OCD Association several years earlier, prior to our respective divorces. Reconnecting with David at this time sparked feelings in both of us, and this became a match made in heaven for us. We started dating and fell in love with each other.

John was able to get to know David and was more than willing to share me with David. He knew in his heart this man would provide a great deal of stability for us and, although he didn't like not being the center of my world, this was an easy decision for him. John's only stipulation was that we didn't get married because of my previous 100-day marriage with my bar manager. David and I were both fine with that arrangement.

John was still my priority and David took John's emotional problems very seriously. David also spoiled John every chance he could. I know that spoiling him could be viewed – especially by the Italian males in the family – as his downfall, but when all is said and done, we must do what our heart tells us to do and not follow the loudest voice in the crowd. (I know souls about to incarnate choose their mother-to-be from the other side of the veil for the way they will raise their children, even if they don't raise them by the psychology of the day.)

After his death, I severely questioned myself on my position of being lenient.

Chapter Five

Adolescence Arrives in All Its Glory

It wasn't long after John started Junior High that I began receiving calls from the school because of his outbursts and truancy, which resulted in many parent-teacher conferences. John had become very hard to handle and was expelled from school. He had to attend what is called "Opportunity School," which is a school for students who are expelled from the regular school system for behavioral problems and truancy.

John Sr. decided he could do a better job than me of parenting and wanted to try. We were all at a loss as to how to help John, who was in desperate need for any kind of attention from his dad, so he moved into his father's house. I saw him often during that time he stayed at his father's house, but on September 19, 1998, I got a call all mother's dread. "John has been hit by a car." I freaked out before I heard the words, "but he's okay".

John Sr. and I both rushed to the hospital, to learn that John's knee was severely damaged. He'd been hit by a car while walking in a crosswalk to get to the school bus. It was before 7 a.m., around sunrise, and the bright early morning sun had blinded the driver.

Because I was a practitioner in the healing arts and a massage therapist, John Sr. let me take my son home with me from the hospital so I could take care of him. Also, I was glad to be able to pamper him again.

That knee injury would play a huge and pivotal role in his life right up until the end, and became a backdrop for many key-learning experiences in his soul growth. I learned later that the car accident was one of four possible exit points[1] for my son.

After recovering from his accident, John was about to experience another trauma in his life. His cousin Joe, my ex-husband's nephew, worked for us as a carpet installer and John was close to him. Joe was a heroin addict who I was always trying to help because of my "need to be needed" syndrome. We let Joe stay with us when he was really sick or we thought he might die. I knew this was not smart and possibly even dangerous for John, however, it was what I know I had to do if Joe had any chance of surviving his addiction. I believe this experience of knowing an addict firsthand was something John needed for the important decisions he would make in his life.

One day, a nurse from UMC Trauma Center called and left an urgent message for me to call her back. It took forever to find out that the call was not about one of my children. I was the registered contact person in Las Vegas for Joe and they

---

[1] An exit point is a prearranged choice point whereby the soul can choose to end the lifetime, such as a serious accident or illness. The soul defines them during the pre-life planning stage, and there are typically five or six in number. This is a concept brought in from many spiritual teachers; I first learned of it during the Spiritual Psychology class channeled from "the Group" through Steve Rother of the Lightworker organization. Steve Rother has taught the Spiritual Psychology class at the United Nations as well as channeled there five times.

were calling to tell me he'd overdosed and was on life-support. I called Joe's mother, Judy, who lived in New York and related this devastating news to her. I picked Judy up from the airport and brought her home to stay with us. Joe was on life-support for over seven weeks, and John watched Judy wake up every morning and try to find the strength to go to the hospital for another grueling day of ups and downs, mostly downs. She never gave up hope that her son would recover, not even on the final day of his life. Joe's physical condition worsened to the point it was obvious to the doctors he wouldn't make it. Judy agreed, on a soul level, to let him go. Within minutes of Judy's agreeing to take him off life support, Joe's heart beat and his breathing began to slow down and he began to die, even without the removal of the life support equipment. I asked Judy and Joe's father to hold his hands and I held his feet and we told him it was okay to go to the realms of the soul. Everyone had suffered enough and Joe needed to travel on.

John grew very close to Judy during that time she stayed with us and saw how much sorrow Joe's addiction caused her. However, the immediate effects on John were very scary. He had moved back home with me from his dad's house and I knew he was smoking pot with his friends. (I found out after his death that the kids in the neighborhood were actually doing way more than just smoking pot). All I could do was ground him. Keeping him from his friends was the only way to keep him from smoking pot. He was never disobedient and always accepted being grounded without a fuss. He would just lie on the couch and watch TV.

One day, he saw a documentary about Kurt Cobain (Kurt's birthday was the same as John's) and he had died of an apparent suicide. He watched this over and over, and I knew he was thinking of killing himself. John began to say such things as, "Everybody thinks I'm just like Joe and I'm going to die just like him." He would also hit himself in the face with his shoes and cry, "I'm nothing but a piece of shit." (These were the words he would use to cry himself to sleep with for the rest of his life whenever he was going through an emotional time.) I would also find sharp knives stuck into the wall through the sheetrock.

I took John to counselor after counselor, only to hear them say, "He's severely depressed and there's nothing we can do for him." His body had such a bad reaction to the medications when he was a child that no doctor wanted to try the "medication route" again. I decided to go see my friend Cattel who channels her guide, Ray Mund. Channeling is the act of serving as a medium through which a spirit or energy connects or communicates with a living person. I became concerned that John might harm himself or if he was in danger because of his severe depression. She said, "Yes, he is in danger. I'll give you some Reiki exercises to work with his higher self."

We did the exercises religiously but everything I tried to do to help him failed. I felt in my heart that he might die if I kept him grounded from his friends any longer. His depression was extreme and I needed to do something extremely different. His sadness was so severe that I began searching for answers anywhere I could find them. Although I never really believed in astrology, probably because I was told growing up in Catholic school it was a sin, I decided I would look to the stars for answers. Michele Avanti, a good friend, is a highly respected, well-trained and published astrologer. Her information about John's birth showed he had several exit points in the coming years and that it was highly unlikely that he would ever live to see his twentieth birthday. I couldn't believe what I heard. Instead of giving me hope, this information added greater fear about his life.

This was not an easy pill for me to swallow, especially because the first exit point was coming up within one month of the reading. We, of course, did everything in our power to keep him safe on that day. David and I took him and all of his friends on a trip to Laguna and then to our cabin in Big Bear. We weren't taking any chances even if we didn't fully believe in the exit point information. The rest of the information had been enough to deeply concern me and I paid close attention to his depression. We made sure that this was a happy week for him ... and it was.

I knew something bright needed to come into John's life and soon, if not immediately. I had lifted the restriction on him not seeing his friends but I knew that that wasn't enough.

I enrolled him in guitar lessons, and he took to the guitar as if he was a natural for it. He practiced constantly at home and would "jam" at a friend's house every night he could. His greatest love was now his guitar and his love for music. I decided to turn the entire garage into a music studio for him and his friends to jam in. He would be at home so I would always know where he was. Having to park the cars in the driveway was a small price to pay for the peace of mind I enjoyed and the great gift of a music studio to my son. David and I furnished the garage with strobe lights, couches, lights and tables and chairs, so it had all the accessories needed for my "up and coming music star." My plan had worked and he was no longer depressed. He loved the studio and jammed there every night possible.

The spring came in with new hopes and challenges as the teen years were getting into full swing. I had just worked at a spiritual fair, giving free demonstrations of Reiki. At this fair, I worked with a woman, Julie, who told me of a modality developed by a Dr. Kenneth Fabian that she believed helped her stay alive and survive after her diagnosis of being bipolar. She piqued my interest and spent days teaching me so I could use this technique with my son. It is called "Deep Feeling Contact" or "Bonding". It seemed too simple to work but I was going to try it anyway. The process involves using your left eye to look intently into the left eye of the "unbonded person," as the website calls "the subject," with an intense emotion of sadness. (This was also known as "Soul Contact" and Steve Rother teaches this technique in one of his seminars.)

The process works by activating the emotions to begin the maturation process. This should occur naturally during the initial bonding process between mother and child in the first few days after birth. Of course, in John's case, I didn't get to hold him until twelve days after his birth and he was blindfolded, so the time for the natural bonding process was over. Dr. Kenneth Fabian now has great success using this process exclusively with children with autism.

John's outbursts were getting worse by the day and his humiliation after his episodes was destroying his self-esteem. Clearly he did not want to behave that way and felt extremely bad whenever he did, so Fabian's therapy was worth the try. My plan was a "five-dollar bribe" for a "one-minute experiment." Since it was the long Easter weekend, money was an easy bribe. The experiment was planned for Holy Thursday and Julie was going to witness the technique to be sure I was doing it properly. The day arrived and everything went according to plan. John was "Bonded" and out the door he went to hang out with his friends. John's 15-year-old cousin was spending the weekend with us because her mother was out of town on business. She told me she would be interested in the experiment if she could also have the same "five-dollar" financial reward. Her birth had been even more traumatic than John's and her emotional development seemed stunted as well. I didn't see any harm in "Bonding" her as well, so I did the same process with her and then forgot about it.

The next day was Good Friday and all the kids were out of school. I had a one o'clock massage and was in my healing room. (Since I didn't charge for my massages, I worked out of my home.) John told me that he and his friends were going to the mall and the niece who I'd "Bonded" said she'd be close by in the neighborhood, visiting friends. Just as I was finishing the massage, John burst into the massage room screaming that my niece was in the middle of the street unconscious and that a neighbor had called an ambulance. Apparently, she'd been drinking vodka and was almost dead of alcohol poisoning. I was naive about how much drinking and drugs were being used at that time by all of the kids in the neighborhood. Within a month of this incident, a warning appeared on the website NOT to use this procedure with teenagers. The website had only previously warned to keep a close eye on them. I didn't realize the danger I'd put my son and niece in.

On the positive side, after we'd all recovered from the trauma of that weekend, John was able to control his emotions enough for us to live a more normal life. We could finally go out in public without the fear of a scene, and I never received another bad conduct report from school again. As a matter of fact, he actually got an "A" in conduct after that. To go from 64 parent/teacher conferences in one year to an "A" in conduct the next is no small miracle. We were also finally able to go out to eat together as a family and take vacations without fear of his behavior problems. We even scheduled a trip to Disneyland in Florida for his next birthday. He was still an argumentative spirit, and always loved to make a point, sometimes too loudly. The difference was that now he could control himself. He was choosing to do that instead of acting without control. He was pleased about this, and no longer felt ashamed after an outburst.

I have used this procedure of "Bonding" many times since with incredible results but I avoid "Bonding" anyone in the teenage years because of what happened to my niece. I still highly recommend that clients learn more about this procedure. In those days, Energy Medicine and its exponential power were still a long way from my comprehension, but my using this simple procedure did not go unnoticed. Dr. Kenneth Fabian gave me a beautiful gift in Bonding that became a foundation I could build upon. I am forever grateful to him and to Julie, who introduced me to his work.

Chapter Six

September 11, 2001, New York

On the surface, all was well. I enrolled John in an on-line school where he could take academic classes from home using his computer. That took a great deal of stress off of me. Getting John to school each day was always the hardest part of my day. For John going to school was like putting him in boiling water every day. I would drive him to school and watch him enter the building. At lunchtime, he would leave the school premises and go hang out with his friends. I did not know where he would hang out and that always weighed heavily on my mind.

Facing the opposition from John Sr. about computer learning from home took a great deal of courage on my part because he felt John would play his guitar instead of concentrating on his schoolwork. Of course, he was right and I knew this, but I also knew that John's passion was to play his guitar. John liked to learn on the computer and always got good marks if I could get him to actually do the work.

My life was busy taking full-time care of my friend with Parkinson's who lived in our home 24/7, volunteering at the

St. Therese Center doing massage and taking aura photos. I was also having some health challenges that had begun in February. Basically, it was that my menstrual period never ended. All tests showed negative for cancer but nothing could stop my bleeding, not even strong doses of progesterone.

Also, the family was in extreme turmoil over the merger of J & R Flooring with a company owned by someone who seemed to me to be "less than reputable." I had relinquished my shares of the company to my children in hopes the company would live on for generations to come. Although I now had no legal or financial interest in the company, the emotional shock to my children over the merger was severe. I had no choice but to "stuff" those emotions and pretend this merger didn't bother me. Many of us have no idea what else to do with painful emotions except to "stuff " them as we have all been taught.

As usual, another fabulous distraction was about to occur to take my mind off the merger. My niece, Jen, had a major roll in a play called *No Mother to Guide Her* in a little theater in Tribecca, New York. Closing night was Monday, September 10, 2001, and John, David and I had tickets for that night. We were to arrive on September 10th, check into the Marriott World Trade Center, watch the play and leave the following day – Tuesday, September 11th.

Except for some really scary dreams I was having about that trip, I was looking forward to it, and focused on the positive things in my life. Another life-altering moment was about to occur. My daughter Michelle blessed us with a rare visit to our house. Michelle and I were sitting on the couch when John came out of his room and boldly announced, in no uncertain terms, "I'm not going to New York." I quickly asked, "Why?" Michelle didn't wait for his answer and said, "I'll take his place." And it was done.

A minor complication surfaced in that Michelle's stepson, Gino, would be turning seven on Sunday September 9, and she had planned a birthday party for Gino on that day. Michelle asked, "Could we change all the reservations, mom so I can have the party for him Sunday?" She asked this casually, as if it was no big deal, but for me it was huge. First, the airlines are a pain in the you-know-what when you're using frequent flyer miles to book a flight. Second, the theater was so tiny that it would take a miracle to get new tickets for the last Friday night performance. Miraculously everything was changed and this new schedule was actually going to work out better for Jen because on the last night of a play, there is a cast party and we would not have been able to spend any time with her. This was no small miracle; in fact, it was "A Really Big Miracle," but we didn't know that then.

Michelle and I arrived at the hotel in the Marriott World Trade Center on Friday, September 7th, along with my sister Diane and brother-in law Danny, Jen's parents. Danny worked for Blue Cross and his office was on the 27th floor of the World Trade Center (WTC). As I walked into the building, I began to hemorrhage heavily. In fact, very heavily. I headed to the nearest restrooms that were only a few feet away in the Tall Ships Bar. (The exit in this bar became the main exit through which thousands of people would flee the tower only four days later. So much debris was blocking the other exits that people were diverted through this doorway in order to get out of the building, despite falling bodies and chunks of concrete.)

Once we left the building for lunch and a tour of the area, I felt better. Back then, I never took photographs, but that day, I bought a throwaway camera and photographed many sites of and near the twin towers. I even took one in the subway when we were approaching the terminal at the World Trade Center.

When we arrived at the theater that night, I had the strangest uneasy feeling during the entire time I was inside. I was trying to concentrate on the play so I could discuss it later with Jen but the strange, foreboding feeling was overwhelming. (The next play that would be performed in the theater would be months later, and it would be The Guys, the story about the FDNY firemen who died on 9/11 helping others starring Sigourney Weaver and Bill Murray and was written by Anne Nelson.)

Saturday morning arrived and we all met for breakfast in a coffee shop located in the basement under the World Trade Center and then spent some time shopping. If we'd kept the schedule as originally planned, we would have been in that basement when the planes hit.

Then we wanted to go to the top of the tower for a view of New York City, but it was closed due to fog.

We got to the airport in plenty of time for the 12:50 flight from Kennedy. In the restroom at the airport, I commented to Michelle that once I'd left the WTC area, I had stopped hemorrhaging and my bleeding was back to normal.

On Monday, I realized I was really weak and decided to see a homeopathic physician for answers to this continuous bleeding problem. I thought maybe the bleeding could have been caused by the transdermal medications from the AIDS clients I massaged or maybe the oil I used during my massages was affecting my hormones. I knew traditional medicine had no answers so I was guided to search in another direction. This one decision on my part changed so many lives that I cannot begin to count, not the least of which was to be my son's life. I made an appointment at The Nevada Clinic for September 24th but was told it would be a longer delay if I wanted to see the founder, Dr. Fuller Royal. The charge for the appointment was about $700, and normally I would have baulked at the cost, but I felt compelled to keep the appointment.

On Tuesday September 11th, I woke up like the rest of the world to the shock of an airplane hitting Tower One. We actually couldn't remember which tower Danny worked in even though we'd just been there. One by one, my sisters and children arrived at our house to wait for some news about Danny. We watched the news for any information about whether anyone from as high up as the 27th floor had made it out of the building, but none came. By the time the second tower fell, I was convinced Danny was dead and asked David to get cash and start packing the car for a trip to New York. My sister Diane would be alone in New York and I needed to get there for her if Danny had died. On hearing my plans to go to New York, John became completely hysterical, rolling on the floor and screaming that he didn't want me to leave him but that he was too afraid to come with us.

I had never seen such terror in him, so I called my other sisters who lived closer to New York and pleaded with them to drive to Diane's house. I promised John that I would only leave him if he and I both agreed it was safe for me to go and ONLY if Danny didn't get out alive. It felt like an eternity before we finally received the news; "DANNY GOT OUT AND HE'S WALKING HOME"! We shed tears and shared hugs of joy for a while until the reality set in that our joy would not be shared by thousands of other families who had not been so blessed that day. We were the lucky few who cried tears of joy before the tears of sadness for the many who were not so lucky. Our sacred world was not shattered or violated because we still had Danny. Our family is exceptionally blessed because we are all very close. After our parents died, that closeness became much stronger. If one member of the family is hurting, we are all hurting.

With Danny having evacuated the building safely, we were able to watch the news with a different perspective from those who had lost someone and different still from those that had no loved ones at risk that day.

So many thoughts now ran through my mind, such as the warning dreams before I went to New York, the last minute change of our travel date to New York and the fact that I bled so heavily only while in the doomed building. I wondered if my intense hemorrhaging had been a premonition of what would occur only days later. And why did it stop as soon as I'd left the building to go to the airport? On the night following the disaster, I dreamed that Diane and I were standing in line at the Armory in Manhattan with Danny's hairbrush to deliver DNA to identify his body. I knew he was alive, so why would I have such a dream? Was it an exit point for him that he chose not to use? The dreams I had before I went to New York were of Jen, Michelle and me running and yelling at Michelle to take off her high-heeled shoes so we could run faster. Other dreams came back to me and I began to wonder if, on a soul level, we all had exit points but changed our plans so as not to be there. And could we actually make those changes in our lives?

Many of my friends are gifted channels and mediums so it wasn't long before I booked a session to get some answers about 'if" and "how" these things might really be possible. I saw Cattel, who channels her primary light guide Ray Mund, with a list of questions I needed answered. Ray Mund basically confirmed that David, John and I, as a soul group, had originally decided to leave this world together in the 9/11 disaster but that at an even higher level, we had decided it was not for our highest good to leave at this time. She also confirmed that early in the planning stages, Danny had also planned to leave and that, too, had been changed.

Every year since the 9/11 disaster, we have a family day on 9/11 and Danny recounts the events of that day. You can hear a pin drop when he begins. Even the babies sit quietly as if they know, on some level; a sacred event is being relived. When Danny tells the story of that morning when he left the World Trade Center after the first plane hit, he always includes the fact that for some unknown reason that day he decided not to go down for his usual second cup of coffee. He is so ritualistic about his second cup that he would have been in the elevator at the time the plane struck Tower One. Everyone in the elevators died instantly because of the burning jet fuel that spilled into the shafts. The elevator shafts became channels for the fuel and huge fireballs blasted up and down them. In fact, the colleague with whom he usually went downstairs died in the elevator and he would have been with her.

I believe, on a level of which our conscious mind is unaware, we choose our exit as carefully as we choose our entrance and for whatever reason, Danny changed his plan at the last minute.

Both Michelle and John wrote very sad songs as a way of processing their sadness. Michelle wrote a beautiful song about the pain of the families of 9/11 and sings that song every year on 9/11 at our family day. John's painful songs were carefully hidden and not to be found until after his death. He had even deleted them from his computer hard drive so they could not be discovered until after he had crossed.

Chapter Seven

My Purpose Becomes Clear

Finally, September 24 arrived, the day of my appointment at the Nevada Clinic. I especially hate doctor appointments but knew this one was necessary. I arrived at 9 a.m. and a nurse gave me a series of tests. The Heart Rate Variability test and then a Voll machine test confirmed that things were not good. Dr. Royal himself, the founder, entered the room and explained that his son-in-law, with whom my appointment originally was, had to leave and so I was placed in his hands. He re-did the Voll test, and joked, "I'm retesting because I don't trust women." Actually, I think he re-tested me because my test results were so bad that he had personally taken over my case. (After the session was over, Dr. Royal disclosed to me that the life force reading on the Heart Rate Variability test was a "16" and anything below a "20" is considered a near-death number).

Then he asked me to trust him and do whatever he instructed. Under normal circumstances, those words from a doctor would be a big red flag but he was the kind of man I found easy to trust. He began asking weird questions and did not seem impressed by my brilliant theories about the oil and medicines from the AIDS patients affecting my hormones and causing me to bleed. He asked about my childhood, my first marriage and if I'd ever almost bled to death. I found that question unusual and told him several times during the session, "Absolutely not." (Of course in the car on the way home David reminded me that I had almost died when Jamie was born because they couldn't stop the bleeding following placenta separation. How our memories work or don't work. They are so incredibly unreliable.)

Next came the really weird stuff. He would ask me to think of how I felt about something. He had me rate the level of my intensity feeling about it from one to ten and then he started tapping on certain acupressure points on my face, under my arm, under my collarbone and on my hands. He would keep checking the intensity of the emotion and keep tapping until the intense feeling was down to a one or was gone. He had me think about both of my parents to see if there were any emotional scars still affecting my life. He asked me to think about the sorrow of my dad's death.

When he asked about my first marriage, I began crying uncontrollably and could barely breathe. He re-tested me on the Voll machine, and I could see he had a "back to the drawing board" look on his face. Then he said, "I want you rub on this spot under your left shoulder and say three times, "I deeply and completely accept myself even if I don't want to get better."

My reaction to this strange request was clear. I thought, you're nuts and I'm not going to say anything so stupid, especially when it isn't true. If I'm spending $700 for the appointment, it's because I DO want to get better. When I refused to say it, he was sweet and patient with me but insisted I needed to trust him on this if I was to get better. So even though I didn't have my heart in it, I said what he asked me to say. He re-tested me on the Voll machine again and said my meridians were back in alignment. He told me I would be fine, gave me two homeopathic remedies and sent me on my merry way. I was quite upset because I didn't believe he'd actually helped me.

It wasn't until the next day when my bleeding stopped completely that I even considered I might be getting better and that Dr. Royal had actually helped the bleeding stop. Two weeks later when I returned and he re-tested me on the Heart Rate Variability machine, I was at "85."

After two weeks of not bleeding and feeling noticeably better, I decided to look up on the Internet what Dr. Royal actually did, but I couldn't even understand the explanation in his pamphlet or the information on the Thought Field Therapy website. By "coincidence," a class in Thought Field Therapy was being taught by Susanne Connelly the next day in Las Vegas and there was room in the class.

I took my aura camera (a special camera that can photograph electromagnetic fields) to the class so I could see if this therapy really worked. After I took the class, I was blown away by what the aura camera showed and by the science that was behind this therapy. I began tapping on everyone who would sit still, but I must admit that tapping on people is not an easy "sell." People cannot grasp that something so simple can have such amazing effects, and even fewer people ever realize the full impact of a tapping session. They don't see their improvement as a result of rubbing on the thoracic duct or sore spot, as everyone in the field refers to it, and saying such things as: "I deeply and completely accept myself even if _____ (name the problem, say, I'm angry at my mother)." When we do this, we are collapsing a subconscious belief. Even fewer realize the full implications of a program embedded in the subconscious.

(It took over a year after my session with Dr. Royal to remember that I had named myself after St. Rose of Lima as a confirmation name. She wore a crown of thorns under her habit so she would slowly bleed to death. I used to study the lives of the saints and be so upset because you couldn't be a saint anymore or die a martyr. If I could have become one, as a child I would have applied. I was obsessed with being a nun and had my sights set on being a saint. The bleeding from which I almost died twice was a big clue to me about my subconscious martyr syndrome.) I might have wanted to die in the twin towers to fulfill my childhood wish of being a martyr.

I became obsessed with this tapping technique because, with my aura camera, I could see the energy shift in people with the use of this modality. All negative emotion is a disruption in the energy field. The aura photos, which are able to reflect these energy shifts, gave some validation to the clients who came to me for sessions. I began studying every modality linked to the entire field of Energy Psychology. I took classes directly with many of the founders of each of these modalities, and couldn't get enough education or practice in the field. I just knew I could help John with this so my heart was in it all the way. Of course, getting John to let me help him was going to be the hard part.

Soon, I have given countless sessions using Thought Field Therapy (TFT) but there were only a few instances where John would let me work with him. The first memorable time was when he was age 15, and a "five-dollar bribe" and good timing could work wonders. One day, John was upset over two things. He was mad at his dad for something and he was upset that his guitar playing was not coming along as well as he wanted. He wanted to be playing like his dad yet was still playing like a kid trying to be good, so he was willing to have a session with me. I had just finished reading Emotional Self-Management by Drs. Peter Lambrou and George Pratt. They had taken TFT to a whole new level, kicking it up "another notch." I was eager to try this therapy on someone and John was the perfect someone. It was going to involve much more rubbing on the "sore spot" and many more phrases, so it worked out perfectly for both of us to experiment. The phrases all began with: "I deeply and completely accept myself even though." I had him verbalize a whole series of phrases that covered as many negative subconscious programs as possible. First, about not being a good guitar player and secondly, about being mad at his dad. He went through it very quickly so he could leave and hang out with his friends. But he actually did it with conviction with the hope he could really be a great guitar player.

He was probably thinking that having a session with me was an easy way to earn money. All he had to do was read a page and rub a spot under his shoulder – easy money. After the session, I dropped him off at his friends and asked him if he was still mad at his dad. He said, "I was never mad at dad. I just feel bad for him." It was as though he'd completely forgotten he'd been angry.

It wasn't long before my daughter told me, "I can't believe how good John plays guitar. Even his dad was blown away by how good he has become." Each year, J & R Flooring has a huge Christmas party, a tradition started in 1983. Each year John, Michelle and John Sr. play a set of music at the party. It became the highlight of John's life to play alongside his dad, still his hero when it came to music. Of course, I knew what had happened to John. His old programs of "not being a good enough musician" were gone, replaced by new programs of "being great" now embedded in his subconscious. I knew he was born with extreme talent hidden within his genetic code and the tapping had activated this talent. If I tap on myself to be a great guitar player, I would still have no talent, however I'm sure I could learn to play guitar a great deal faster than if I didn't tap. There is an obvious difference between learning an instrument and having a special gift. That tapping session was a real turning point for John and it only cost me five dollars plus the cost of the book. Emotional Self-Management, at that time was one of the best books on the subject because it addressed the subconscious programs better than most others on the subject. At this time there are a number of books about tapping and I have not read them all.

As I mentioned earlier, John would rarely let me work with him. He was a tough cookie when it came to getting him to do anything. He had something called "Oppositional Defiant Disorder" and he had it bad. As I researched more about "Attachment Disorder," I found that many of the symptoms are the same. Again, the birth trauma of being isolated from touch, no eye contact and being tied down might have played a huge factor in him having the disorder.

The next memorable time I worked with John stemmed from an outright threat on my part. It was before a trip to Michigan to see my niece, Amy, play an Indian in Peter Pan at the community theater in the Kalamazoo Civic Theater. My reservations were made but not John's because he would never commit to fly. This was due to his severe phobia of flying. When he finally decided to go, I only had enough points for a coach seat for him so we would not be sitting together on the flights. Him sitting alone did not bother me because his behavior was always at its worst at airports and while he was flying.

The day before the planned trip, at his sister's birthday party, I noticed his anxiety level getting high. When we returned home from the party, I told him, "If you don't let me tap on you, you can't come with me." I'd never forced a treatment on him before but I knew he was getting crazy because of his anxiety over flying. He seemed relieved that I forced him into it because, this way, he didn't have to ask mom for help.

After we tapped on the flying anxiety, I could see his whole demeanor change. If we tapped out anxiety, we needed to fill the space with a new positive program. You can think of it like deleting an old version of a program in the computer and installing a new version. He told me he wanted to fly first class with me. Being an optimist, I said, "Okay, let's do it!" He envisioned sitting next to me in first class on all six flights, three in each direction between Las Vegas and Kalamazoo. We tapped it in and I was curious to see how he would do. He was in an exceptionally good mood preparing for the trip, and I kept teasing him about what he'd done with the "Real John."

At the airport, Delta Airlines informed us there was NO WAY they could upgrade a ticket purchased with points. John didn't get upset, saying, "See, it didn't work." He remained in a good mood and just took it in stride. I, of course, checked again with the agent at the gate for an upgrade ticket and received the exact same response. On the plane, John went to his seat in coach and I went to mine in first class feeling really guilty. Just as they brought me my wine (to ease the guilt), the agent walked up to me and said, "There's no reason your son should not sit next to you since we have an empty seat."

When I went back to coach and told John, he had a huge smile on his face that set the tone for the most magical weekend. I know this is hard to believe but the same thing happened on all six flights! Now the Irish will never let the truth stand in the way of a good story, but this is the truth.

When we got off our last plane in Michigan, snowflakes the size of half-dollars were falling and John was in his glory. He tried to catch them in his mouth and played for a long time in the snow. He loved both the snow and his Michigan cousins, Amy and Matt, and that trip became one of our best memories.

Chapter Eight

More Lessons for John

Although years passed, John's knee never completely healed. It was obvious that I was the overprotective mom, but his dad wanted John to be a man, lay carpet and just forget about his knee injury. Being a massage therapist, however, I was more aware of soft tissue injuries, so I took John to the best sport doctor I could find, in hopes he would tell us that John shouldn't lay carpet, but the doctor agreed with his dad. His exact words were, "We will never know if his knee will hold up unless he tries to lay carpet."

John went off to work every day that summer and I made him tell me if his knee hurt. Every day I would call the doctor to tell him about the pain John was experiencing and what actions were causing it. The doctor would tell me that the knee was fine and the pain was to be expected. It soon became clear he did not even want me to call, so John finally stopped telling me about the pain.

Naturally, being on his knees all day laying carpet ended in disaster for his knee. When he finally admitted he couldn't stand the pain, his knee had deteriorated so much that he needed a complete soft tissue replacement. The surgeon apologized and admitted he didn't like me and that his judgment to let John continue to lay carpet was poor. That was huge; at least he was honest. He referred us to a specialist for that particular type of surgery because it was so complex. John was especially upset that they would use a cadaver for the replacement ligament.

On the day of the operation, David and I waited in the "pre-op" area with John while they prepared him for surgery. John had IVs in both arms and they were getting ready to move him on the gurney into the operating room. Suddenly, John had a panic attack so severe that he started pulling his hair and screaming to me that he was losing it. The nurses were shocked and tried to hold him down and put ice on his head. To make matters worse he ripped the IVs out and blood started shooting everywhere. With all my training, I knew that if I tapped under his eye, it would calm him down but the nurses were blocking me from reaching him. They were at his bedside and trying to hold him down. I pushed my way to him and tapped under his eye. Within seconds, he said, "I'm okay, mom."

It wasn't until after John's death that I did research on birth trauma and cell memory, and realized that his reaction in pre-op stemmed from being tied down in the incubator for so many days after his birth. In addition to being tied down at birth, he had a compounding trauma at the age of three. He'd split his face open and was rushed to the hospital for stitches. They had to put him in a papoose, which enabled them to strap him down and keep him still when they put the stitches in his face. The nurse who held him down nearly smothered and crushed him in order to keep him still for the doctor. Knowing that his face could be scarred for life, they needed to keep him as still as possible when applying the stitches. John naturally became hysterical at the sight of the needle going into his face.

We were totally unprepared for the level of difficulty he would have from such an extensive operation. I spent the entire six-week period spoiling him, and we had a great time with movies and treats galore. David got him a mandolin, which John began to play instantly without any lessons. John's physical pain was severe but he handled it as best he could.

Once again the emotional trauma would be the worst part. Because he couldn't lay carpet, he was treated as a failure in the eyes of his father, which only made him feel even worse about himself. The new surgeon said he would never have allowed John to lay carpet, nor could he even now. John lost any hope of gaining his father's respect. If he couldn't lay carpet, he'd never be treated as anything but a useless kid whose father owned the company; a stigma he desperately had tried to avoid.

During his six-week recovery, no one on his father's side even visited him or sent him a card. We all live within a mile of each other so visiting him posed no hardship. It might have gone unnoticed except my family showed up daily with everything and anything to make his life better. In other words, we all spoiled him rotten. This dichotomy was what made it worse.

To really put the finishing touches on the self-image of failure, John Sr. put John on the payroll and said he need not show up for work. I seemed to be the only one who saw that the absolute worst thing to do was pay John to not come to work. (Prior to birth, we each set up our life plan for that particular incarnation, with all the lessons we need in order to learn certain things. Ironically, we humans learn better from painful, negative experiences than from loving, joyful ones. John had a lifetime of experiences, both good and bad, crammed into only 19 years.)

While sitting in a recliner for six weeks, John had time to discuss his future with me. One of the things he'd decided to do was to take his GED exam, which he passed with flying colors without ever opening a book. He applied to several music colleges. Everyone was giving him advice and helping him with the requirements for the applications. He had researched various music schools and had narrowed the list down to two. One was in Los Angeles; the other in New York. David and I took him to a music college in Los Angles but he decided against going to that school so John Sr. agreed to take him to Five Towns College in New York.

The Five Towns College in New York required two additional parts to accompany the application. One part was to compose an original piece of music. After John wrote his song and had practiced it for several days, I filmed him playing the song and so he could critique himself. The second part of the application required that he write a letter to the school as to why he wanted to attend that school.

The required letter he wrote to Five Towns College as part of the application was beautiful. It read:

"I have played in a family band for years and have done well in local talent contests. The guitar is my main instrument along with the mandolin and the dobro. Songwriting and re-cording are my favorite pastimes. Playing to my pets even makes me happy when I see their reaction. My family comes from Brooklyn, New York and I always wished I grew up there. I have visited several schools in California but I feel more drawn to New York, especially Five Towns. Five Towns College is the only school I am applying to because the school I choose is the most important decision in my life right now. I am currently taking three music classes at CCSN and also private lessons this semester. I have my own little recording studio and enjoy playing and recording with my friends. One of our recordings was chosen for a school documentary. Music is the path I have chosen for my life's work. Although my family has an established business that I can earn a sound living at, my heart would not be in it. My family has ties to music

that trace back several generations. Music has been part of my life as far back as I can remember. So many areas of music interest me along with the desire to play as many instruments as possible. My goals are to perform and compose. I am drawn to jazz and to music that heals. Since I have also been exposed to negotiating contracts, the business of music holds great interest for me as well. Loyalty to my family and friends are important to me. Music has a way of getting the truth out to many people and can change the world for the better. My music is the greatest gift I can give back to the world."

He put his heart and soul into the application.

It was only days before going to New York to audition for the college and the last thing he had to do was to take the ACT test.[1] However, the night before the test, he had a fight with his father and John said, "Well, that's the end of that dream. The trip is off. My father said I would never get into college because I'm not good enough."

I didn't know if that was said or not. John was so sensitive that he could misinterpret anything. At least two of his teachers recommended him to the College, so he knew in his heart he was good enough. I begged him to take the ACT test anyway. He didn't even need to do well on it but just needed to take the test. Some schools make special allowances in academics with low ACT tests scores, if the student is exceptionally talented.

He went to take the exam but came home an hour later in tears. If his life lesson was to feel like a failure, he sure planned it well. His heart was broken and I knew it was going to be hard to put him back together again.

---

[1] The ACT® test assesses high school students' general educational development and their ability to complete college-level work. It consists of multiple-choice tests in English, mathematics, reading, and science, and an optional writing test, which measures skill in planning and writing a short essay.

John Drives

John had resigned himself to not going away to school that fall and decided to buy a truck. Because of the high rate of teenage accidents, I suggested John get an old truck for a year and then he could have any car or truck he wanted. He willingly agreed to this and bought an old Ford Bronco. About two weeks after he got his license, he got up on Sunday morning and told us, "I'm going to pick up Derek, a friend, and drive him home." If the guys in the neighborhood were partying on a Saturday night, they would crash wherever they were that night and find a way home the next morning. John was excited to do this.

Two minutes after he left the house, the phone rang. He had hit a light post and needed me to come right away. By the time I got there, traffic was backed up because the Bronco had caught on fire and then finally became engulfed in flames. Four fire trucks were on hand, putting out the fire, and no traffic was moving because of a police barricade around the entire area. The column of smoke seemed to be a mile high in the sky. The first thought David and I had was that John had gone back into the truck for his CDs just before it became consumed in flames and that he'd been killed. David told me to get out of the car and run to the scene because we couldn't drive through the police line. As I left David in the car, I could see him make the sign of the cross. Of course, in the back of my mind was the prediction that John wouldn't see his twentieth birthday. Finally as I approached the scene, I couldn't even recognize what had once been a Ford Bronco. A police officer saw the panic on my face and asked if I was "Mom." The police officer pointed over to the grass and I spotted John sitting there safely about a hundred feet away. He was immensely relieved to see me.

John later explained, "After I hit the post, the truck spiraled out of control and Derek didn't have his seatbelt on. The passenger door flew open and Derek held onto the door through the open window as he swung outside the truck. The back wheel came off and the truck almost overturned onto Derek. As soon as the truck stopped, we got out but the sparks from the wheel that came off started the fire and then the truck became a fireball."

John realized how close he came to killing his friend. The truck would have crushed Derek if it had flipped onto its side. Apparently, John had looked down to change the song on the CD player and wasn't paying attention. When he looked up and saw the light post, he tried to turn but the side of Bronco bounced off the light post. When I was teaching him to drive, I must have yelled at him a thousand times for changing a CD and not watching the road.

This close call reminded me of the astrologer's awful prediction about his early exit and I was constantly holding my breath about that. However, John did become a much more careful driver after that. The next purchase was a brand new truck and it wasn't long before his next accident, which wasn't his fault. He was rear-ended by a police officer because John slowed down for an ambulance to pass and the policeman did not. John suffered a severe neck injury, which took three months to heal enough for the doctor to release him for work.

On July Fourth, the day before he was to return to work, John dove into the swimming pool and hit his head hard on the bottom. His head wound was streaming with blood and he re-injured his neck. He went back to the same chiropractor who took x-rays and the doctor told John he had a concussion and more damage to his neck, so he couldn't go back to work for at least two weeks. Not only did this news receive no sympathy from John Sr. but it also was the straw that broke the camel's back. John Sr. unloaded like never before about what a disappointment John was and basically told John he never wanted to see him again. This was the worst fight the two of them had ever had, and John stayed in his room for three days. I was starting to worry, but got him out of his room by convincing him to go to the beach with his friends. This prospect cheered him up, and he started to plan the trip. In fact, John became famous for his trips to the beach.

I took an aura photo of him the day before the trip and I could actually see the chair he was sitting on. It was as though he was a transparent ghost. I totally freaked out and immediately showed the photo to Cheryl Johnson, my favorite psychic. "Is John in any danger?" I asked. Cheryl did not know anything about the exit point prediction from the astrologer, and to my horror, she said, "Absolutely yes, he's in danger."

"So what can I do?" I asked.

"You have one chance before he leaves to convince him that everything his father said about him was not true. Now to make it very convincing, you need to approach this differently than you ever have before."

The approach I decided to take was to show him that just because someone says something, it doesn't make it true. I asked him, "Do you believe everything your dad says about me?" He answered, "No, I don't," and saw where I was going with this. "So, just because someone says something about someone, does that make it true?" I asked. He shook his head, and I asked, "How many times has someone said something about someone that you knew wasn't true?"

That was all I could come up with. I felt I'd made the point, and gave him over to Mother Mary, entrusting John's safety to her.

John went on the trip and made it home safe one more time, and I was very happy and relieved.

Chapter Nine

2004: We Discover the Healing Power of Sound

John was still enrolled in the Community College taking music classes. His friends were going there, which made it a fun thing, and he loved music so it was a win-win. He started working selling cellular phones but it required standing in a booth all day, and standing all day was not good for his knee. The knee surgery had failed and he needed to have a second operation ASAP. Also, he had difficulty working in the tiny claustrophobic box in the Wal-Mart store. Each day before he went to work, I worked with him to ease his anxiety. He was determined to make it work and submitted to the daily sessions so he was able to leave for work. He absolutely did not want to fail or it would mean that everything anybody had ever said about him being a failure was true. I was proud of him for sticking it out.

On Saturday, August 28th, I was scheduled to teach a class in Energy Medicine in a beautiful retreat house called Almost Heaven in Mt. Charleston. The date was rapidly approaching and the response to my seminar indicated I might have more participants than I had planned for.

On Sunday, just six days before the class, I ruptured the S2 disk in my spine. Luckily, I knew of a website that had a tapping sequence for every ailment known to man and since the class was about tapping, what better way to learn about this site? Barely able to move, I had to slide out of bed and slither down the stairs to the computer. I went to the web site for Attractor Field Therapy at www.the-tree-of-life.com. looking for the appropriate tapping section. It was much more complicated than Energy Psychology. Since I could barely move because of the pain in my back, I was trapped at the computer and had no option but to tap my way out.

After I finished the recommended series of tapping, to my surprise I could get to the couch. The pain wasn't completely gone but this was a huge improvement considering the fact that I was sliding on the floor an hour before.

The next day, my back was still painful. I had trouble walking and lifting, which was a problem because I had to carry all the bottled water from my car into the house, organize the chairs and tables, and move all the furniture around in order to get ready for the seminar. In other words, I had a problem and needed to see substantial improvement. I was still tapping for 30 minutes a day so I could at least walk during such a busy week.

I printed out the entire 80-page website on Attractor Field Therapy so I could sit on the couch while I tapped. The printout of the website mentioned a CD and a special antenna that would emit a frequency throughout the house that would do the same thing as the tapping. All I had to do was put the CD into a boom box, insert the special antenna in the headphone jack, so that the antenna would block the sound and convert the sound to a signal. I could press REPEAT and wouldn't have to tap anymore. The signal from the CD-player would run a constant 24/7 tapping session through the whole house.

This sounded too good to be true, but I was desperate … and I'm also quite lazy.

The tapping I had to do for my spine and my pending hectic schedule was more than I could handle so I decided to give the CD a try. I called the telephone number on the web site to place my order for the "basic" CD and to my surprise, the founder of Attractor Field Therapy, Dr. Kurt Ebert, answered the phone. I couldn't believe it, and had so many questions. Tapping was my passion and I could pick the expert's brain before I taught my class. What luck! He sent me the "basic" CD overnight. I received it on Tuesday and put it on REPEAT overnight. When I woke up the next morning, my lower back was perfect. I was completely cured, and amazed I was in no pain at all.

John was in a really good mood because the basic CD I played all night sent waves through the entire house thereby treating everyone in the house and because, the previous day, he had negotiated a large settlement from the insurance company for the accident that had injured his knee.

Dr. Ebert called, wanting to know what I thought about the CD. I was rambling on and on about how I thought this was the greatest thing on planet Earth and couldn't believe no one knew about it. I told him I was going to order more program CDs – one for John's knee, one for his learning disabilities, and one for his panic and anxiety disorder. I told Dr. Ebert, "I'm definitely going to discuss the CDs at my presentation on Saturday". He then asked, "How would you like me to do a presentation at your class?" I was dumbfounded at what I'd just heard. I accepted his generous offer and reorganized my class around him.

This would be a miraculous event and I was excited because Dr. Ebert would allow me to film his presentation. I felt I was in heaven, sure in my heart that this new therapy might help John's knee, which above all was still my greatest concern. All the money in the world couldn't fix his injured knee but maybe the CDs could. Since I drove Dr. Ebert everywhere that weekend after picking him up at the airport, I was able to pick his brain, which for me was a huge gift. I loved what I did (Energy Psychology) and was full of curiosity about its full implications for body, mind and spirit.

Dr. Ebert's presentation was fabulous, and I could barely stop thinking about what these CDs could mean for humanity. I had visions of these giant antennas raising the vibration of humanity. (I'm always looking to make the world a kinder place.) Sound waves were the new order of healing and research for me. Overnight our lives had been transformed.

On the Monday following the event, John asked me, "What do you want from me as a 'Thank you' for all you've done for me. You can have anything you want." He figured I would want to go on a cruise, but to his surprise, I told him, "I want to do research with the CDs and I want the set of all forty of them." This was going to cost over $2,000 but he was feeling generous. I had interviewed 15 attorneys for his final negotiations with the insurance company and he was very aware of the time I'd spent and the impact my efforts had had on the outcome of his settlement.

The check from the insurance company took about a month to be approved because closing a lawsuit requires a lot of paperwork to be filed with the court. John and I went together to pick up the check. He didn't need me to go with him but it was our special time together. We always had lunch together or an ice cream after all of our appointments, and today would be no exception. With so many frustrating trips to so many doctors and lawyers offices, we finally had a happy trip together.

David became his financial advisor and John trusted him with all his heart. David respected John and vice versa. David was there for him to talk to, and John was extremely worried about doing the wrong thing with the money. He was conservative and didn't want to waste it. He told me after he deposited the check, "If anything happens to me, this money goes to my nephews for college." I know if I received a large settlement, I would have squandered a great deal of it on myself.

Every dime John spent was to make someone else feel good or to help his friends and sisters. He had set $700 aside for a large family Texas Hold'em Tournament, and couldn't wait for the game. That game was all he talked about from the moment he finalized his settlement until he picked up the check. We went directly from the lawyer's office to the gaming supply house to buy a set of professional Texas Hold'em chips and cards. Our family always had fun on those nights. On the day of the tournament, he overheard a friend telling me she didn't have rent money, so he took half the money he'd set aside and asked me, "Would you give it to her but don't tell her where it came from." It didn't matter to anyone that the pot size went from seven hundred to four hundred. It was a glorious night regardless of the size of the pot.

When the set of all the Accutone CDs arrived, I bought a stereo with a five-CD changer. I picked out the best five CDs to play in the house for John. I wasn't sure what all of the 40 CDs were for but I experimented with them nonstop, not only with John but also with all my clients. Most of my clients felt great benefits from them in whatever area was needed, be it emotional or physical pain.

The most memorable healing was a woman who was in agony because of constant migraine headaches. Although the CD for migraines did not help much, the neck and brain damage CDs made her feel much better. For John, the leg and foot CD was a priority as we were still trying to figure out what to do about his knee. Again, to my complete surprise, his knee felt better after playing the CD. The CD for Oppositional Defiant Disorder, anger, panic and anxiety were also always on, which noticeably helped him with his emotions.

Shortly after school began again in the fall, John had another crisis. He was failing his Music Theory II class. His self-esteem plummeted because he felt he couldn't even pass a subject he loved. Without his knowledge, I played the learning disability CD and his grades went from a D to an A in just one week. He was thrilled about himself and so was I. I never told him I'd played the learning disability CD, because he would have taken that as an insult.

His knee was still a problem but he decided he was not going to have another operation. The CD was working well enough to get him by but did not completely fix the knee problem. One day at school, his knee gave out and he fell. He had to be carried to the car, which was very embarrassing for him. After the fall, he became very careful with his activities to avoid any more problems.

Going to concerts was a problem because of the walking and jumping involved but he just dealt with the pain. This meant he couldn't always sit with his friends because he would often have to walk a distance to the good seats, but sometimes he would just suffer the pain if he really loved the music.

Once again, John Sr. pressured him to start laying carpet. His father could never quite get it that working on his knees all day was out of the question. Every time his dad and I spoke on the phone, we'd have a confrontation about why I wouldn't let John work on his knees.

Even though I couldn't have stopped John, he knew better than anyone that his knee simply couldn't hold up, especially after the operation had failed so miserably. But because

John had never complained to his dad about his knee pain, John Sr. just didn't believe he had a problem. One of the reasons John probably didn't complain about the pain is that I think he was self- medicating. It was easy to get pain medication from the kids in the neighborhood. He easily could have gotten his pain pills from his doctors with the shape his knee was in, but I think he wanted to hide the fact from me that he was taking them. He didn't hide the fact that he drank and smoked pot but he figured I'd really get upset if he was taking pills, as well.

Chapter Ten

Nine Months Remain – A Reverse Pregnancy

As I look back now, these last nine months were so intense with the final preparations for his leaving – it felt like a reverse pregnancy. I spent nine months preparing for his birth and now I would give him back.

Christmas 2004 was over and it had been a good one. Two really wonderful things happened that season. First, I was invited for the first time since 1993 to the J and R Flooring Christmas party. My daughter Jamie now solely owned the company, and my children really wanted me there. Being the ex-wife, I was obviously not welcome at prior year's parties while John Sr. owned the company. That had now changed, so I got to see them play and it was a huge thrill for me. No one could have dreamed that it would be the last time this would ever happen. What a wonderful gift that was for me.

Another wonderful gift was that John, David and I adopted one of the local charities and gave them a fabulous holiday. I was working with the social workers for the State of Nevada in my sound research. One charity I worked with was the Oasis

Center, a residential program for children with emotional problems that made it hard to place them in foster homes. Working with individuals with emotional problems was right at the heart of what I loved to do.

After one of the sessions with a housemother, I asked what Christmas was like at the center. To my horror, she described a very sad tale. Because of a state law, the employees cannot solicit funds or donations for the center. The state provides a gift certificate of $50 per child each year and that's all the children receive. I knew that Las Vegas was an extremely generous community and other Las Vegas charities receive large donations at Christmas, but these poor kids had slipped through the cracks. For example, Child Haven, a more temporary shelter for abused and abandoned children, gets a great deal of attention and donations thanks to tennis star Andre Agassi and many other generous patrons. Child Haven always gets publicity during the holidays from all the local TV stations. I asked one of the housemothers to get a "wish list" from each of the children. Together, John, David and I, along with all of David's generous associates and Susan Erling, a very generous friend of mine, raised enough money to more than fill their "wish list." We bought brand new computers, new carpet (donated by my daughter Jamie), plenty of "impossible to get" X-boxes, and truckloads of gently used clothes and toys. The Oasis Center had a fabulous Christmas. We also gave them gift certificates for various stores near the center that lasted through half the following year.

We received the names of each child at the center and John had a special gift for each of them. He put $40 in each envelope, sat with each of them, looked into their eyes, hugged them and wished them a Merry Christmas. This experience had a huge impact on him and he cried in the car on the way home, for he wanted to do much more for them than just give them money. I talked about him giving them guitar lessons and how much they would love that because they loved the karaoke machine we had given to them. He said, "I don't think I'm a good enough teacher."

Soon Valentine's Day came and Oasis Center invited us to a thank-you party in appreciation of the Christmas we'd given them. The kids went all out to show their thanks, each writing a thank-you note for the individual gift they had received. Also, they made a large 3 x 5 foot poster for all the group gifts we'd given the center.

Before we even knew about the thank-you party, John had mentioned he wanted to do something special again for the center. I told him, "I'll pick up hearts filled with chocolate and cards for you." He insisted, "Go to 'Sees Candy' in the mall. I want them to have the best chocolates available. And can you get enough cash for another cash gift for each child."

As I mentioned before, I hate the mall but of course I did what he asked, complaining all the while I stood in the two-hour line. I could have bought the chocolate hearts at Target in five minutes (I guess there are still remnants of my martyr program). John insisted, "If I'm going to give them something, it's not going to be crummy chocolate."

Again he was so moved by the way these children were growing up without parents and he couldn't get over it. John had connected with one young man at Christmas, and asked why he wasn't there. He was told, "He wasn't allowed to come to the party because he's being punished."

This was incomprehensible to John because he was never really punished as a child and felt that just living at the center was punishment enough for anything the young man had done. I explained, "With so many children, the rules and discipline have to be enforced to keep any kind of order. These house mothers do not have the same luxury of spoiling the children that other people do."

For the first time in his life, John realized just how lucky he had been his whole life and how easy his life was in comparison to theirs. He even saw his relationship with his father from a whole different perspective. He began to see things, not as a spoiled child with a knee problem, but from the perspective of one who had much to contribute to this world. He became grateful for everything good in his life and started saying, "Thank you" constantly. He always said, "I love you, Mom," but the added flavor of gratitude was especially nice. I was proud of him and who he had become.

One night in February, I got up around three and couldn't go back to sleep; a common thing among women my age. I was flipping through the TV channels and came across my favorite movie of all time – *The Singing Nun*. We all have a fantasy life and mine was to become a nun. I just knew when I first saw that movie I would someday be a missionary nun in Africa. The movie was at the part where she sings the hit song Dominique on the Ed Sullivan Show. In real life, the singing nun was a Dominican nun and she wrote the song in honor of the mystic, St. Dominick, one of my favorite saints. In 1214, the Blessed Mother gave St. Dominic the Rosary as a weapon to win a war. I quickly recorded it and watched it several times until I felt tired and went back to bed, happy to have seen the movie again. I even showed it to David after breakfast the next morning and I told him of my silly fantasy life.

Later that day, John came home and said, "Hi, Mom, I want to introduce you to someone special. This is my friend Dominique." I couldn't believe the coincidence and asked her if she'd ever heard the song Dominique. She said she had heard of it, but never actually heard the song, so I immediately put the movie on and made the poor girl sit right next to me as we watched it. She must have thought I was nuts and I'm sure John felt embarrassed. He was very precious when he introduced his new girlfriend to me, and I had high hopes for a girl to come into his life and settle him down. I was worried about John becoming addicted to alcohol (an Irish tradition) or worse, and hoped that she would have a good influence over him. I loved her right away and was in awe that she was named after the mystic and saint that presented the Rosary to the world. My dedication to the rosary and Saint Dominic was such a large part of my faith. This was going to be a happy time for all of us. I could just feel it.

Chapter Eleven

So Much to Be Experienced in So Little Time

John Buys a House

On a beautiful Sunday morning in March 2005, John came downstairs in a great mood and said, "Let's go look at houses." This took me by surprise because I didn't think he wanted to leave us just yet. We let him get away with a lot, gave him the spare room for a music studio and never complained about his messy room or the constant activity of musicians coming and going.

David was going to work that day so I said, "Sure, that would be fun." I could tell John was in such a good mood that we would have a good time just being together. We drove toward the beautiful Red Rock Canyon, where only new homes were being built, all of them super-nice. The new and luxurious Red Rock Casino Resort and Spa was being built nearby and John loved that area. His love of the Red Rock Canyon was as strong as mine, and we often hiked in the park with my daughter Michelle.

As we passed the Red Rock Casino and Spa, he asked me to turn into the first development. The sales people told us they had only three houses left in the development and they were willing to negotiate in order to sell them that day because they were closing the sales office the next day and moving it to a new location for another development.

The three houses had fallen out of escrow but the prices were more than what John had in the bank. He wanted to look at them just for fun, and fell instantly in love with the first one he saw. It was the perfect floor plan for him, with an unobstructed view of the mountains from the master bedroom balcony. There was no way the view could ever be blocked. John didn't understand about finances but when I told him he couldn't possibly afford the house, he started to question whether he could get a mortgage and, if so, whether he then could afford to buy the house. David owned a mortgage company and was a real estate broker, so I called him and asked him to come to the house right away.

Long story short, David, being a total deal junkie, negotiated a fabulous deal for John and cosigned on the mortgage. This was going to be great for John, who couldn't have been happier. He felt that real estate was a good investment and, if he had all of his funds invested in real estate, his friends and relatives couldn't borrow any more money from him. He could say in total honesty, "All my money is invested in the house." Many things fell into place for him and he started working again as a "runner" at J & R Flooring to earn extra money to pay the mortgage. (A runner is the person who delivers invoices, picks up plans and does whatever else may be needed, one of the most important being getting his sister Jamie's Starbucks orders.)

On the first morning he awoke in his new house, he called and told me he was still in bed and could see the beautiful mountains. He was excited and so incredibly happy, and wanted me to thank David for all he had done to bring about this wonderful gift in his life. I knew that he didn't have a washing machine yet, so I would still see him once in a while. This helped me get over the empty nest syndrome.

The Wedding

David and I had many spiritual marriages over the years but we honored John by waiting for our wedding. We wanted a fairytale event and planned it for May 1, 2005. David and I designed the entire wedding ceremony as a tribute to the Blessed Mother. We were totally caught up in planning, and since everything in our family is about music, the music at our wedding was going to be a big deal. I asked my sister and my children to play at the ceremony and the rehearsal dinner that was to be held at The Irish Pub in the same hotel where we were to be married. I arranged to have them play and use the pub's sound system for an hour before the Pub's regular band started their routine. This was fine with the pub manager because my sister, Teresa, had a lot of influence with him.

John started practicing the music he was going to play, which was very important to him as he never was allowed much input in the planning of the songs at the J & R Flooring Christmas parties. Also, he was never allowed to sing; his father and sister sang all the songs at the parties. Although he was well respected by them for his guitar abilities, they didn't feel his singing was up to their standards. This was going to be his vocal debut and he couldn't wait.

As we were going over our wedding plans, John played a song for me I'd never heard. It was *Ripple* by the Grateful Dead, and was the song he'd chosen to sing during the ceremony as his gift to us. As I listened, I was a little puzzled. It was upbeat but didn't seem like a wedding song. I know now that in his heart, he knew he was leaving this earth and began dropping clues of his departure. The last ten words of the song are: "If I knew the way, I would take you home," where "Home" is actually heaven. The message in the song was clear: he knew even then he was leaving. The family practices of the songs for the wedding and rehearsal dinner never occurred because my daughter's fiancé had a very serious accident, which took the focus off the music for the wedding.

The Saturday night before the wedding, John and my sister sang a few songs for the family. I knew his singing meant a great deal to him but everyone could see that he was not doing well. I was even concerned he would not make it to the wedding. Of course he did make it and walked me down the isle.

At the wedding reception, he and I had the traditional "Mother and Son" dance to the song, *You are the Sunshine of My Life*. He was really happy for us and had a great time at the

wedding. The wedding was videotaped, and I am incredibly grateful to have those films and photos. I hold those moments so tenderly in my heart. All I have to do is think of that dance and I can feel John holding me again. I saw him the next day and felt sure in my heart he'd be okay until I returned from my honeymoon at the end of May.

When we returned home from the honeymoon, John looked good. He came over and picked up the gifts we bought for him and Dominique at the various places we'd visited. He was happy that I had bought something special for Dominique. I knew he had very strong feelings for her and that they were spending a great deal of time together. I also had high hopes that she would put her foot down about his drug use. I knew if anyone could influence him, she could. I was extremely relieved to see John was safe.

That night, I had one of those "real" dreams you can remember every detail of. In the dream, John was killed in a car accident and I had to go to the morgue to identify his body. When I arrived, I knew he was dead but he didn't. He was laying on a table and asked me, "Am I still alive?" I had to say, "No, sweetie, you're not." He then asked me, "Why did I have to die"? At that point I woke up crying hysterically. I woke David, which I never do, and told him about the dream. The next day, I was still so upset about the dream that I told my sisters, describing the dream in every detail, right down to the shirt he had on and the blood on his face.

Saturday morning about eight o'clock, the phone rang and I was relieved to see John's name on the caller ID. He was crying, and told me, "I ran a red light and hit a car. I think I'm probably going to jail. If I do, will you promise to bail me out?" David was still sleeping so I had to summon up my courage and go to the accident site alone. My fear of the police was still very strong, even though I've tapped myself a lot on that issue. I drove in a state of complete surrender to Archangel Michael, who I knew was John's main protector.

When I arrived at the scene of the accident, I was relieved he was okay and no one was hurt. He mentioned to the police he'd been drinking the night before. They never even asked him that, but he felt so guilty that he just volunteered the information. After he'd said it, the officer had no choice but to cite him for drinking under age. He got two tickets, one for running a red light and a second for drinking under age. He was not issued a DUI because whatever alcohol had been in his system was gone. He couldn't believe they didn't arrest him. I was just as surprised.

I was relieved that he'd miraculously escaped another planned exit point. I was holding onto the thought that this was a sign he might live past his twentieth birthday. I was counting the days because his birthday was only eight months away.

During those last few months before his death, John always seemed to be in crisis. As I look back, it was as though once he made the final decision on a soul level to leave; he needed to accomplish many things.

The next crisis in his life was that his friend Alex, who was now living in John's house, was addicted to heroin and the prescription painkiller Oxycontin. Alex had been living on the streets since he was a young teenager prior to moving in with John. He was an incredibly talented drummer and was a regular in John's band. Alex was robbing the neighbors for money to buy drugs. The robberies became so frequent that John was torn between keeping quiet and letting the robberies continue, or asking one of his best friends to leave the house and not return. John's principles could not allow someone to injure another knowing that he could stop it (a trait that he inherited from me) so this gave him the courage to protect the neighbors from further theft, so he asked Alex to leave and not return. This was difficult for him.

Spiritual Psychology

In July, I took a Spiritual Psychology class given by Steve Rother, founder of the Lightworker organization and a channel for some nonphysical beings known simply as "the Group." During this one-week seminar held here in Las Vegas at the Tropicana Hotel, I was fascinated to learn that before we incarnate, in order to fulfill our life plan and lessons, we-the-soul preplan all the major events in our lives. Also, many of our life lessons are directly tied to abuse or lack of love on the part of one or both parents. It was a wonderful class and I couldn't get enough information about our pre-birth plans and "contracts."

According to the Group, a "contract" is an agreement made between two souls that govern the interaction between their respective incarnations. This gave me such a different perspective on John's relationship with his dad. Whatever their contract, I had no doubt that their relationship was playing out exactly as they had planned it at the soul level.

I'm sure I needed to be reminded of these truths to prepare me for forthcoming events. On the fourth day of the seminar, the entire class traveled to the Almost Heaven retreat house in Mt. Charleston for a channel by Steve.

An unusual thing happened during the channel. The Group stopped Steve in the middle of the channel for a reason he could not say, and instructed him to leave the mountain right away. As the channel ended, I became so overwhelmed by sadness that I couldn't speak or move. I began crying uncontrollably from the core of my being for no apparent reason. Being shy, I just stood on the sidelines hoping I wouldn't be noticed. Finally, I made my way over to Charmaine, one of my dearest friends, who had helped me at all of the events I gave up there. She also runs the Lightworker office.

She took one look at me and knew I was in some kind of trauma. She put her arms around me and cried with me until I finally stopped. It was an experience so profound I could not even begin to grasp it. (To this day, I don't understand what happened to me, but the unusual events at that retreat house had only just begun.)

It was not easy to get out of my mind what had happened but the days of the class were incredibly intense, which helped me put the crying trauma behind me.

On the last day of the class, I went to breakfast early and alone at the Tropicana Hotel coffee shop, intending to go over the prior day's material in order to integrate all I had learned. This material rang true for me and was important for the work I do. However, a number of people from the class soon joined my table. I often stay to myself in the classes, so I was thrilled to get to find out about my fellow classmates.

One woman, Janee, was sitting across from me and I asked her what she did. As normal as anything, she said, "I do Light Language."[1] My soul responded with such excitement that you would have thought I was an expert in it. Even Janee was in shock that anyone else knew what it was.

When I asked her where she lived, she replied, "Well, I'm not sure." This was not an answer anyone expected to hear, so she had the attention of everyone at the table, especially me. She explained, "My life path led me to this class and I will be guided to know my next step by the end of the seminar. I have placed myself in the hands of the Universe."

---

1   It is a heart language that speaks only truth. It raises the energy of Mother Earth and all who hear it.

My history of taking in weary travelers along life's path is far too long for just one book but I had promised David now that we were married and finally alone, it would stay that way and I would not bring people in crisis home to stay with us. It was still less than three months after my promise, but David was not at all surprised when I told him I wanted to bring Janee home with me for a few weeks. Bare in mind that those words, "A few weeks," have meant as long as ten months on other occasions. Janee moved in with us that weekend.

Janee and I were having a great time and David grew to love her as much as I did. One day, when John came over to visit us, Janee sang Light Language for him and he wanted to record her on his computer. We talked about making the recordings at the Mt. Charleston retreat house as soon as he'd fixed his computer.

Janee's stay with us was less than a month as she found her next lamppost on her path of life and moved in with Tony Stubbs, my editor and the editor for Lightworker Publications books.

John's Message from St. Michael

One Tuesday morning, John called, quite frantic. Someone had severely damaged his garage door and he wouldn't leave the house until it was fixed. He didn't want to be late for work, and was basically freaking out. He didn't explain why someone would damage his garage door, or who, but I had my suspicions. He didn't have the nerve to call Jamie to tell her he'd be late for work, and asked me to do that while he called a garage door company.

Jamie said, "It's a slow work day, so tell him he can take the entire day off." John was always afraid we were mad at him, so he was thrilled she wasn't angry with him missing work.

"Hi, are you mad at me?" was a question he'd ask me ten times a day for absolutely no reason. He also did the same with his girlfriend, Dominique, and his sisters. That funny greeting was how he started a sentence. It was just a "John thing."

After the door was fixed, he called to ask if he could take me to lunch. After he received his settlement, he treated me whenever we went out. Buying me lunch was his way of saying thank you and letting me know he really appreciated everything I did for him. He really loved doing that, and used to tip the valet parking attendant a $20 bill. When I asked him why he tipped him so much, he would just reply, "It makes me feel good to make his day better."

We met at Claim Jumper, my favorite restaurant. His first words were, "I've got something to tell you and it's going to blow your mind. You're going to think I'm crazy." Then he realized, everyone thought I was crazy, and we laughed. He told me that, out of the blue, the garage door repairman told him he had a message for him from St. Michael. "St. Michael wants to warn you that you need to make a change of direction in your life right away or something bad is going to happen." I asked, "Do you understand what the repairman was talking about?" and he replied, "Yes," but didn't want to talk about it. I knew if I pursued what it meant, John would get upset, so I let it go.

John had an altar in his house with his favorite statue of St. Michael and another of St. Francis in the center. It was the focal point of his living room and the first thing he put in the house. He asked me to have my friend Susan, Paul Faulkner's daughter, make him a special Rosary for the altar. Susan makes healing necklaces out of crystals. John knew how devoted Susan was to Mary and wanted the full protection of the Blessed Mother in his house. Somehow he felt if the rosary were made especially for him, it would hold special power. It still amazes me that the only thing he ever asked of me for his house was a Rosary. This is not a typical nineteen-year-old's request.

The previous week, Latifa, another of my psychic friends, had asked me for John's cell phone number. At lunch, John asked me if I'd given Latifa his number. I nodded and asked him what she'd said. "She said if Alex comes into my house ever again, it would be very bad for me." He then assured me, "I will never let Alex back in the house again. I know what I have to do. I'm also going to get off all pills right away. With my garage door being vandalized, I know changes are my top priority. I feel honored that St. Michael cares enough about me to send a messenger." I was surprised at his honesty.

John was the only one of my children who could appreciate this kind of experience because he was so sensitive and spiritual. He was more excited than if Dave Mathews, the rock bandleader, had sent him a message. This was a good day. St. Michael was watching over John and we both knew it.

In the month of August 2005, things started to speed up. Looking back now, he had to fit many things into his last weeks of life. He called me several times saying he had to stay home from work because he was sick. He was trying to detox on his own. He would never admit this to me and I let this obvious call for help go right over my head. Dominique kept urging him to tell me the truth about why he was sick but he couldn't bring himself to do it.

He had a huge fight with Jamie, and came to my house early one morning to tell me, "I want to quit J & R Flooring. I just can't stand the thought of being a runner for the rest of my life." We talked about the fact that fall classes were starting again and that being a runner was just a way to earn money and have a job with some flexibility. His sister was pretty lenient about his work schedule and I could fill in at J & R as a runner for him if he really needed time off. If he was going to quit the job, he needed to give Jamie notice so he wouldn't leave her without a runner. She had all the responsibility of her family and the company on her shoulders and she was pregnant. I begged John not to quit his job over a fight. It was not the right way to leave his job.

John and I were having this conversation on my boat. (We live on a lake and had just bought a boat, on which I practically lived for the first few weeks after it arrived. Anyone looking for me knew where I'd be. Later, the boat would become more important in my life than I realized at that time).

Jamie called him while we were talking on the boat and they patched things up. He said he would go back to work the next day, although I knew it wouldn't be long till he would quit his job for real. I just wanted it to be the right way, and for a good reason. He just didn't feel he was of any value just being a runner.

A couple of weeks later, John went on vacation in Gettysburg with his dad, which I knew meant a lot to him so I became a substitute runner at J & R Flooring for him while he was away. This made him feel he wasn't letting Jamie down. He called me three times a day to make sure I knew the best routes to the various jobsites. He worried I would get lost or drive in some dangerous places. He even watched the TV Weather Channel from Gettysburg so he could warn me about any flash floods. He would tell me not to risk my life for the job. During one of his "checking up on me" phone calls, he reminded me how important it was to deliver the invoices to the right person at the jobsite or Jamie would not have a check when she expected it for payroll. I had to remind him I had invented the job before he was born and if anyone knew how important the job was, I did. However, I was touched by his concern and thought he was adorable. We talked on the phone more while he was on that trip than we had ever before.

John was really hurting because Dominique was going to move to Texas, and he tried to explain to me how difficult this was going to be for him. He talked about his future and told me he was going to make some big decisions when he returned from Gettysburg. He was really happy he'd spent time with his dad and felt very good about their relationship.

He never unpacked from that trip. He had plenty of clothes so his luggage just stayed packed until he died. To this day, I have never unpacked it. I'll just have it placed in my coffin when I die. Only kidding!

Back at work the next week, there was already trouble brewing. John was being pressured into taking a trip to Utah for the Labor Day weekend and wanted Friday off. Jamie said, "Absolutely No Way" because he'd already missed so much work. His roommate and best friend, Jack, wanted John to go with him to Utah for his brother's wedding. John was very close to Jack's brother and was needed for the bachelor party. It was a small wedding and an even smaller bachelor party – just John, Jack and the groom.

Jack put pressure on John to leave early Friday morning, and John was seriously torn but I had no problem telling him, "You really need to fulfill your responsibility to Jamie." He even asked me to work for him and I said, "No." In the end, he gave into Jack. He knew things were getting out of control both at his house and at work, so he asked me if he could come to live with me while he figured out what he was going to do with his life. I said, "Yes."

He had a big fight with Jack and told both Jack and the other roommate they had to leave his house. He needed to get away from his friends and he had rented his house to his cousin, Jason. John had a dog, Guinness, an English bulldog, and

David and I didn't want another dog in the house because our own dog, Caesar, had just died unexpectedly and David was still heartbroken over that. He didn't want to go through that trauma again. (I have read that if a young person dies and has no one they know on the other side, a pet will precede them to help them acclimate to where they are. Caesar, the dog that had just died, had lived with the three of us since John was fifteen and had died for no apparent reason two months before John died.) John started bringing guitars and personal things over to our house and we talked about the rules of his return. We made it clear that his friends were not going to "hang out" here again and that he could not jam here. He was okay with that because he wanted to get away from them anyway. I told him he would have to behave as a guest would but he could stay as long as he wanted. Guinness was still an issue but both John and I knew that David would soften after John brought the dog over a few more times.

One day, John told us he was thinking of buying a recording studio with Frankie Perez, a famous musician in Vegas. John had played with him at the J & R Flooring Christmas parties. John asked David to meet with him, Frankie and John's dad about buying the recording studio. David was thrilled that John wanted his financial opinion, especially when John said, "I wouldn't make a move unless you approve."

As things turned out, the studio purchase never happened but it showed that John was thinking about and planning his future.

Chapter Twelve

The Blessed Mother Prepares Me

Although this is a timeline about John, something was happening in my life that was certainly out of the ordinary. My girlfriend Tracy, who owns the Almost Heaven retreat house on Mt. Charleston, asked me to hold another class at the house because she rents it for business functions and wanted to expose business individuals to it. We agreed to meet and talk about the details. She asked, "Could you bring your camera because I want you to see something very unusual. I think the Blessed Mother's image is in the window between the double-paned window in the grand room of the house, and I want your opinion."

This was an odd request but I always enjoyed a trip up to Mt. Charleston. Twenty years earlier, I'd taken a trip to Medjugorje in what was then Yugoslavia, where the Blessed Mother had been appearing to visionaries for years. The country was still under communist rule at the time, so I was asked to smuggle several hundred Rosaries hidden in my clothes into the country. I, of course, did not know they would be pointing machine guns at me while they searched my luggage. The priest who'd asked me to smuggle the Rosaries had failed to mention this minor detail to me. While I was on that trip, many of the pilgrims to Mother Mary's Shrine would see Mary in tiny specs of dust, in their photos or in their bologna sandwiches. I was never impressed with their fanaticism. It always felt like wishful thinking to me and I felt sure the Blessed Mother had better things to do.

Anyway, this trip to the mountain had special meaning to me because Mary had visited the house in the form of an apparition once before. I had been present during that apparition but didn't see Mary. Others saw her, but I only felt her. We were told to ask her for anything we wanted, and my request was that I could live totally in her service. My request was granted. Those of us who were there that day never spoke of the apparition except to a special few.

After seeing the window, it was hard for me to ignore the image, and I took many photos of the window. There were three, 20 foot high, windows and the image was perfectly centered in the middle window. It appeared to have been created by moisture trapped between the two panes of glass. I later uploaded the digital photos to my computer, studied them and printed them. I got so excited about the images in the photos that I made an appointment with my friend, Cattel, the psychic medium. I knew Ray Mund, the primary light guide she channels, would put these images in perspective for me. I also felt I needed to check on John. Cattel and Ray Mund were keeping a close watch on John for me and were always honest and candid about how he was doing.

They knew about the prediction of his early death and always guided me to help him get back on track if needed. I had always spoken of my fears about the possibility of John leaving early, and Ray Mund didn't sugarcoat the dangers in his life. Through Cattel, Ray Mund told me to take the photos of Mary in the window to Steve Rother at Lightworker. This really puzzled me because I knew Steve wasn't Catholic and really didn't think he'd be interested. She said, "Go see him right away. There's still time to get them to him before he leaves town." This last message was even more bizarre. I didn't understand the rush and thought Steve had already left town. Ray Mund simply said, "Mary has her own agenda."

As far as John was concerned, Ray Mund said, "There's a seventy percent possibility that John will be arrested." This caused me to get extremely upset, and I resolved to not let that happen. I asked, "Ray Mund" is there anything I need to know before we end the session?" Ray Mund said, "Just remember to stay grateful." Again I was puzzled because I am always grateful. In fact, I'm often accused of being a Pollyanna and wearing rose colored glasses. Again I just let it go. The worst part was that during lunch, Cattel said, "I have a sense of John's energy feeling a lot like John Belushi's energy." (The actor John Belushi died of a drug overdose.) I didn't comment on that remark either, and it was as though she never said it. Why did I block that out? I never even remembered her saying that until after John died. What part of a mother's consciousness deletes the words that might have saved her son's life? The words will haunt me forever.

My focus that day was the 70 percent chance of John being arrested, and my mind was reeling. Even though we'd hired an attorney to handle the tickets from the accident in May at the court hearings, there was an internal glitch in the court system and both cases had been scheduled at exactly the same time in two different courtrooms. The attorney had only been able to appear for one of the tickets, and the other judge had issued a "failure to appear" bench warrant for John's arrest. Nothing could possibly be worse for John than to be in jail. He just didn't have what was needed to survive in jail. I could have survived, but he wouldn't. It would have made me crazy if John was in jail and I couldn't get him out.

As it turned out, Steve Rother was fascinated by the photos of Mary in the window and immediately put them on the Lightworker website. As a result, many people went up to the house to see the image of Mary and pray at the window. My girlfriend Susan, Paul Faulkner's daughter, who made John's Rosary, went up almost every day. She took a photo of the window that showed the roof of the building gone and trees growing into the building. Steve was really amazed by that photo.

Many people from all over the world commented about them, and Steve asked me if I would be the guest on the Virtual Light Broadcast1 at the end of September to talk about the window. I told him he should be interviewing Tracy, the owner of the house, as it was her place to be interviewed, not mine. Steve was more than happy to interview her too, but he also wanted me on the show. I had no idea why, for I was only the deliverer of the photos. When I asked Steve if it was Mary in the window, he said, "The Group is laughing," which I took as a yes. He added, "Well you called her in." In my mind, who doesn't call on Mary when they are in a crisis? My connection to Mary was very strong but I know that there are millions of other people who are much more devoted than I am, although there is no place in my home or yard where her image is not prominently displayed.

Soon after the photos and the interview were posted on the Lightworker website, I received a call from a woman named Samarah. She lived in Arizona and said, "I'm a channel for Mother Mary and want to know if I could do a channeling at the window. I'll pay my own way." The words, "Of course" flew out of my mouth before I could think, and we set the date of September 14th for her channeling.

I picked Samarah up from the airport and was privileged to spend the next 24 hours with a channel for Mother Mary. I was in my glory and could barely keep my feet on the ground. We had lunch at The Irish Pub and drove to Mt. Charleston to prepare for the channel.

It was still light out when the channel began. Samarah sat directly under the window while she channeled Mary. The transcribed message appears in its entirety in Appendix A and a free download video of the channeling is available on my web site – loveinactioninc.com. The channel was also videotaped, and you can see the image in the window actually change while the channel was taking place. In one photo taken that night of the window, an image of Mary is visible in the form of light.

Samara channeled a full session for Tracy after everyone left and told her to rename the house "Casa De La Paz," or "House of Peace." I think Mary has big plans for that house.

On the following morning, Samarah and I headed back to Las Vegas, stopping first at my house where Mary had a message for David. She told him, "Open a nonprofit organization called Love in Action right away." He did, and it was incorporated on September 29, 2005, just two weeks later. I didn't know that this nonprofit corporation's website would be so instrumental in the future. We felt Mary's urgency for this nonprofit but did not know its purpose. We assumed it was for the tax benefits for those who would give to the Oasis Center.

The web site has since become many things but mostly helps people to understand the benefits of Energy Psychology.

After a quick boat ride around the lake, we headed for the airport, stopping briefly at the offices of J & R Flooring. I told Samarah my children were struggling and asked if Mary would bless them. She waved her hand, almost like a queen would do, and we continued to the airport. I knew a special blessing was on its way, and it was truly in the knick of time. A miracle was to occur within hours. The prediction of a possible arrest actually occurred that night when John had a confrontation with the police.

I made certain that John did not drive until his tickets and the bench warrant were cleared up because I was still worried about the "arrest thing" Cattel and Ray Mund had warned me about. The morning after Samarah left, David mentioned that John had called about 9:30 the night before but I was already asleep. He'd told David not to bother me and he would call me in the morning.

The next morning, John called and told me he had in fact almost been arrested the previous day. Most of his friends hung out in front of his friend Brian's house, which served as the neighborhood stop off. We had lived next door to Brian for several years and everyone knew everyone in the neighborhood. John had driven to Brian's house and as he got out of his truck, three police cars had pulled up. He was handcuffed and held at gunpoint. They told him there was a report of a terrorist with a shotgun in the neighborhood, and John fit his description. John told the police he had a good job, owned his own house and had no record of any kind.

The police were angry and treated him rough; doing everything they could to make him give them a reason to arrest him. They called him names, searched his truck and became even angrier at not finding anything to at least ticket him. (After Cattel told me he might get arrested, I'd warned John to make sure he didn't even have a pipe or rolling paper in his truck, let alone pills or alcohol.) John and his truck were both squeaky clean, which angered the police even more. Just then, a female friend who lived in the neighborhood drove up to see what was happening and they searched her car. She was not so lucky, and the police handcuffed her and gave her a ticket. The parents on the block came out and assured the police they'd known John since he was a child and that they obviously had the wrong person, which again made the police even more furious. Finally, after what seemed like hours to John, they let him go. However, even as they did so, they called him "a piece of shit."

He couldn't believe that they not only didn't apologize, but also foul-mouthed him. He was so horrified at what the police could get away with that he planned to write his next song about it. For the first time in his life, he realized what life must be like for a person in a minority.

John was not nearly as upset about this incident with the police as I thought he would be. He took it as a great learning experience and felt there was a purpose in it. He was much more concerned about what he could do for the people in Louisiana affected by hurricane Katrina. He wanted to start a drive at J & R Flooring for the victims, and planned to talk to his brother-in-law, who was his boss, about it at lunch.

John believed that it's a songwriter's responsibility to teach through music, and his songs show this. One of my favorite songs he wrote is called *Jesus Never Said You're Not Worthy*, about the fact that the Catholic religion teaches us that we are not worthy but that is simply not true. Nowhere in the Bible does Jesus say that. John wrote this song as a gift to me because he knew much of my work is dealing with the issues of unworthiness and self-hatred.

We went to lunch and discussed his future life. He was evaluating some short-term options, such as quitting his job and going to work as a volunteer for the Red Cross. He was also thinking of moving to Houston to be near Dominique because he missed her so much. He was looking into music schools in Houston. He was also thinking of going to Austin, Texas to visit Joe, a musician friend of his dad's who flew to Las Vegas every year to play keyboards at the J&R Flooring Christmas party. Joe respected John as a musician and felt John could make a living running a music recording studio, which was the same work Joe did. But for right now, John's focus was on moving back in with David and me. I told him that David and I were getting ready to go to Sedona for a couple of days and we would be back on Friday, September 23.

On Tuesday September 20, John called me in Sedona to tell me he was worried about Dominique's safety because a hurricane was headed directly for Houston. It was still three days away from Houston so I told him to get Dominique on a plane to Las Vegas right away. I added, "Listen to me for the first time in your life. Do not wait another minute." My ulterior motive was that I just had a feeling this would be a good thing for him. She could help him pack and get out of his house and back home to me, so I was overly pushy about it. He told me I was overreacting and that Dominique would never leave her family.

Later that day, while David and I were still in Sedona, we received a call from a neighbor because our overhead garage door was open. This is never a good thing to hear when you're out of town so I asked John to check out the house and close the overhead garage door. He called back and said, "The only other thing that's unusual is that the boat cover is off." We knew we'd closed the garage door and securely tied down the boat cover when we'd left the house. My mind started working overtime. I asked John, "Which address did you give the police when they handcuffed you?" He said, "Yours. I never changed my driver's license address from your house to mine."

I was really concerned that the police were actually looking for drugs and that the story they gave John about a terrorist was just a cover for a drug bust. I was sure the police had searched our house and the boat for drugs. My mind was racing out of control as I could feel in my heart he was in danger. I called him back. "Listen, John, get all the drugs out of your house NOW."

I just had such a bad feeling that I called my son-in-law, Glen, Jamie's husband and John's boss, and asked him, "Would you go to John's house and tell him what I said about a possible drug bust?" Glen did go to John's house but John wouldn't let him in. Glen felt John was hiding something from him and that there were definitely drugs in the house.

On the next day, Wednesday, we were still in Sedona when John called and said he was upset about me sending Glen to his house. He added, "I need you to come home right away because I need to talk to you." I replied, "I'll call you as soon as we're on the road coming back to Las Vegas."

This was a strange request from John, and we never packed so fast in our lives. Ten minutes later, we were on the road and I called John. "We'll be home in five hours so wait for us at the house." He said, "Okay, I'll wait. I'm okay now, so don't worry." For me not to worry after him asking us to get back home as soon as possible was not exactly possible, but I tried my best. I started reading a book aloud to David to get my mind off of it. The Way of the Master by James Twyman is a beautiful book about St. Francis. John admired St. Francis and his relationship with animals, and I asked St. Francis to intercede for John and keep him safe.

We drove straight through to Las Vegas without a break but when we got home, John wasn't there. When I called him, he said he would come over tomorrow, which was Thursday. He didn't show up the next day but called to tell me he'd talked with Dominique, who didn't want him to come to Texas until he'd been "clean" for a while. This gave me good reason to hope for John's ability to beat his addiction. I knew being with Dominique could be a great incentive for him to stay away from drugs and kick his addiction to them.

Chapter Thirteen

The Final Touches of a Life

Monday morning, John showed up at the house on some kind of pills, and I couldn't stand to even look at him with that look in his eyes. I made him breakfast and told him to come back tomorrow when he was "clean." He felt really bad that I was so hard on him, but to my surprise he showed up on Tuesday morning clean. His eyes were clear and so was his head. He said, "I'll come every day for a session with you until I move back in on Sunday. I want to go to Houston as soon as the planes are flying again after the hurricane." Then he talked again about joining the Red Cross, and about colleges in Texas.

Also, he had severely injured his knee again. He had forgotten to wear his knee brace and his knee had given way. As a result, he'd fallen down the stairs and hit his head so hard that his head literally had gone through the wall. He added, "My head is okay, but I'm more worried about the cost of fixing the wall." I told him I would help him find a good contractor to repair it.

I told him about a new therapy called "Prolo Therapy" that might work without surgery. It strengthens ligaments with injections. It actually deliberately re-injures the knee to allow the body to repair itself. I had researched this therapy and was really impressed with its results. He asked, "Can you make an appointment right away because my knee is killing me, but I am absolutely not going to have surgery again."

In the back of my mind, I was thinking, if he did have surgery again, I would take care of him at my house again. He could completely detox and I would know where he was every minute. That might be a miracle in itself. I also love taking care of people when they are sick and he was my favorite patient. I was very good at making the best of a bad situation. He kissed me goodbye and thanked me for being there for him. He said, "I'll come before lunch tomorrow for the session. I want to take you out to lunch at the Macaroni Grill."

Our session on Wednesday was very productive. In the BodyTalk System, a system of Energy Medicine, which I always use to begin a session, I was instructed to treat John's breathing. John admitted, "I'm having trouble breathing since I hit my head when I fell down the stairs."

I did treat the breathing and after the session his breathing was greatly improved. We were both thrilled that he felt immediate relief. He said, "I don't want a long session today because I'm hungry. I'll be back every day, so let's go eat."

Over lunch, he told me, "You really hurt my feelings by sending Glen up to the house to tell me to get rid of any drugs. Everybody at work already thinks badly about me, and that only made it worse." It's true. The office staff at J & R Flooring is all family members, related either to his dad or to Glen, Jamie's husband. John was very sensitive about what they might think about him and knew this "possible drug bust" put him in a bad light. That's the kind of gossip that the family makes a big deal about. He said, "I'm not mad at you but wanted you to know how hurt I felt that you did that."

I was totally ashamed of myself. He was so sincere and calm, and my heart broke because I could imagine how bad I made him feel by doing this. I had only wanted to protect him from further problems. He knew I was worried about him so he dropped the subject right away. After lunch, as we pulled into the garage, he said, "Mom, this is the first time we had lunch and didn't fight about something." It wasn't that we would really fight. He would just get easily annoyed at something I would say or do. He left, saying quickly, "I'll see you tomorrow."

The next day, I was thrilled to see how clear his eyes were but I could tell he was having a bad day. As soon as he climbed up on the massage table for the session, he started talking about his money. He told me, "I want to put it all in your name so I won't have access to it anymore. I don't trust myself and want to get money only through you."

I said, "I think you're being very responsible and I'm sure you don't need to do that. Let's talk more about it after the session." (I found out long after he died that a couple of people were really pressuring him to lend them money.) He told me his knee was still hurting a lot. I always use the BodyTalk System so I couldn't work on his knee yet. Through kinesiology, I asked his body what to do first and was instructed to first use tuning forks on his neck.

I was trained in the Acutonics system of tuning forks. The harmonics of the forks are tuned to the frequencies of the planets. I often use the harmonics instead of tapping in my sessions because when I use the Emotional Freedom Techniques, this often brings the body into balance faster than just tapping. The forks are placed directly on the body's acupoints. The tuning forks that I used on the neck was a perfect fifth, with the colors blue and gold.

After the session, John wanted to give me instructions about his house. "I want to be sure you would handle everything if I go to Texas right away. I want to be sure the house is repaired perfectly for Jason." I wanted to tell him what the knee doctor had said but he said he had to go and said that we could talk about it later. He kissed me, thanked me and then told me to watch the movie Crash. I asked if it was violent, he said, "Yes it is, but you'll love it." I asked, "Do you know what the harmonic was I used on you?" He replied, "Of course, mom. It was a perfect fifth." He was great with music and I loved that he was coming home.

He didn't come for a session on Friday because he was going to pack all day and get the garbage out of his house. I was happy he was doing that and didn't give it another thought. He asked, "Can you make macaroni for Sunday as a welcome home dinner?" In an Italian family, macaroni is a religious experience and I was well trained. Twenty years of Sunday macaroni made me a pro, even though I was Irish. I shopped for the sauce, which always included meatballs, sausage and pork. My children couldn't deal with even a slight change from the sauce they grew up with. In the years after the divorce though, it was only on a special occasion that I would make a sauce. Christmas and birthdays qualified as special occasions and John's homecoming was definitely high on the list. He'd made it through the toughest part of his life and now would be starting fresh.

That Friday night saw another special event in our family. My nephew Charlie and his wife were visiting Las Vegas for a friend's wedding. We were especially happy to see Charlie because he'd lived with us for the two summers while the Luxor Hotel and Casino was being built. He was in college majoring in construction and we got him a summer job working for Perini, the contractor building the Luxor. Charlie was the light of our life during those summers due in part to his amazing sense of humor.

Most of the family was meeting at one of the best steak houses on the strip for dinner with Charlie and his wife. When

David and I picked them up at the airport, Charlie asked how John was. I simply said, "He's great, he's moving home with us on Sunday but honestly I need a Valium every time the phone rings." I was only kidding but he got the picture.

This dinner was interesting on many levels. My sister Teresa, who is a promoter and lobbyist, was working on a difficult legal situation involving Paul Faulkner (the man who saved John Sr.'s life 23 years earlier). Rarely do our interests connect, but as I mentioned earlier I'm very close to the Faulkner family and was really concerned about the outcome. Also Susan, who made the Rosary for John, is Paul's daughter and an officer of the company having problems. Every member of their family was going through a rough time due to these matters. Teresa and I spoke briefly in private about the status of the problem and continued with our family dinner back at the table. Teresa knew of the strong connection between the Faulkner's and me so she put great deal of time and care into handling this project.

The second important thing that night was that orbs (spherical angel-like beings that can show up in photos on special occasions) showed up in almost every photo taken that evening. The only other time I had seen an orb in a photo was at John's 19th birthday party.

The third thing of great importance was that the men in the family discussed whether I should do an intervention with John on his addiction problem. They obviously had no idea how hard John and I were working on his problem, but it did alert me to get John out of Vegas as soon as possible.

On the morning of Saturday, October 1, 2005, I was running errands early that morning and called John to see if he wanted to go to breakfast. I was near his house and could pick him up. I told him David thought we should take a trip together right away so he could detox more easily away from his drug-using friends. John liked the idea of us taking a trip and asked where we could go. I rattled off many places we could go without a passport; such as the many cruises we could take and mentioned Hawaii as a personal favorite. I begged him to let me pick him up as I was now even closer to his house and I knew I had his attention. He said "No, but I'll stop by your house later today to talk about it." I said "I'll be home all day making sauce for tomorrow. Janee and Tony are coming for dinner and we're going to have spaghetti. Feel free to have dinner with us."

When I arrived home, my daughter Michelle was there. She was moving out of her house into a smaller place until her fiancé was fully recovered from his accident. I mentioned to her about the idea of an intervention and she agreed I should just get John out of Las Vegas, and then left.

Later John called me furious. He asked, "Why did you tell everybody I was addicted to drugs. The whole world thinks I'm a drug addict." I explained, "I didn't. I only asked Michelle if she thought we should get you out of town for a while."

Somehow, my conversation with Michelle had gotten back to John. I asked him, "So, are we still going away?" He replied, "I don't know," and hung up on me. I knew he was upset but assumed he would just show up in the morning as planned. He usually cooled off in a little while.

Tony and Janee came for dinner, and afterwards we ended up sitting on our boat having deep discussions about life. It was a new moon and the sky was pitch black. I was taking random photos into the night sky, and was able to photograph an occasional orb. Tony suddenly said, "Take a picture over there." I did right away as though there was some urgency. To the eye, there was nothing but a black sky, but a very bright light showed up in the viewfinder of the camera screen. Even before I uploaded the picture into the computer I could see the bright light in that picture but nothing visible in the sky. Tony and Janee asked me to email them that photo in the morning. The next morning, after cropping the photo, I saw that the bright light had the shape of an angel with a giant orb right next to it. I emailed it to Tony.

David and I then decided to secure the boat moorings for the fall. While we were doing that I mentioned to David that I was worried that I didn't put enough breadcrumbs in the meatballs. John was pretty fussy about the meatballs. We were both still on the boat when I heard someone call my name.

I was about to learn, in the most painful way imaginable, of the significance of that bright light in the photograph the night before.

Section Two

The Focal Point of the Tapestry

Chapter Fourteen

A New Form Is Taken

I turned and saw Jack, John's best friend and his mother, crying and running towards us through the gate of the backyard. The instant I saw them, I knew the moment I'd dreaded since that astrology reading was here. Jack was screaming, "I'm sorry. It's all my fault."

I asked as calm as I have ever spoken, "Is he dead?" After Jack said, "Yes," I asked, "How?" and held my breath. I needed to know above all else that John didn't suffer. The answer to this question was more important than anything else to me. Jack fell to his knees and then sat on the step with his head in his hands, sobbing uncontrollably. Between sobs, he said, "John didn't wake up, and it's my fault."

I hugged him and told him, "It's not your fault, no matter what happened. John and I both knew he was going to die and it was only a matter of how. What ever happened was not your fault."

Jack's mother was crying and David was sitting on the boat with his head in his hands not yet able to move. It took a long time for Jack to stop crying so I could do what I knew had to be done. Finally, Jack was able to explain why he felt it was his fault. "I took Alex to John's house with me from a concert last night. I knew Alex was using oxy, and he begged John to buy him five oxy to hold him for a while. Another reason it's my fault is because John asked me to let another friend, Sharon, come over to spend the night to help him stay off drugs until he made it to your house. I objected to Sharon coming over because she and I had had a falling out and I told John I didn't want her around."

So I asked, "Where is John now?" Jack led me to believe that the police had already been to the house and John's body had already been removed. My first call was to the morgue, and I learned they had no record of him. My sister Teresa is a good friend of the Coroner, so she was my next call. I told her, "John has died from an overdose but we can't find his body, so could you start calling? I'm going to John's grandparents' house to tell them what happened and get John Sr.'s phone number so I can let him know what happened."

In all of this, I had not yet cried a tear. I just needed to take care of telling John's father and sisters, and find my baby. I needed to find my baby. The terror of seeing his body kept me from breaking down. I was paralyzed in fear. Nothing scared me more than what I was about to face. I knew it would fall to me to identify his body. I had done it my dream and was terrified.

I had just finished reading the book about the life of St. Francis and *Living with Soul*, the book by Tony Stubbs. These books reminded me of what I needed to know in my heart to get through the next few days. There would be no blame. I did not even blame myself at this point. (There would be plenty of time for that later.) Each of us could trace back to something we should have done, or not done, that would have changed what had just happened. I knew Mother Mary had John safe in her arms and he would never cry again in pain.

David drove me the few blocks to John's grandparents' house. Even after the divorce, I stayed on friendly terms with them. His grandfather opened the door and his grandmother was in the bedroom. I asked him to get "mama," and told him something terrible had happened. She came out and intuitively knew whatever I was going to say was too horrible to hear. I asked her to sit down and she just kept saying, "No, no," as though if she didn't sit down and if I didn't speak, she wouldn't have to know.

This was when I could no longer hold back the tears and knew I wouldn't make it through the sentence without crying. The dam burst and the first of a million tears began. We cried together for a long time. His grandparents lived in our guesthouse when John was born and they were a big part of John's life until the divorce. I knew they loved him dearly. I also knew the divorce was difficult for them as well. I knew this was only the first of many difficult encounters awaiting me. After what seemed like forever, I asked for John's Sr.'s number and to get him on the phone. I truly cannot remember what words I chose but I was kind and so was he. I told him the numbers he could call to stay informed.

I still had to find my baby. Jamie was out of town on a camping trip and Michelle never answered her phone, although I called her several times without leaving a message because I just didn't know what so say. I left a message on Jamie's husband's cell phone to call me right away. I wanted Glen to break the news to Jamie, especially since she was pregnant and this would be such a shock for her.

Just as I got back to my house, Teresa arrived and said she'd had no luck finding John's body. There was no record of him anywhere. Just then John's cousin Jason called to say, "I'm at John's house and the police are waiting for you. They haven't taken John's body from the house and they need you here right away."

Teresa, David and I went to the house and found the neighborhood filled with so many cars that David had to park a block away. As I walked into the house, many of John's friends and some of their parents were in the living room. The police were polite and asked me to identify John's driver's license. They asked if I was his mother and if I had ID. I answered, "Yes" to both.

John was still upstairs so I started to go up. The police officer told me, "That's not a good idea. Why is there nothing in his bedroom but the clothes he's wearing?" I explained, "He packed up everything to move back to our home this morning." They asked very few other questions. Even though this could possibly have been a crime scene, it was as though they didn't try to investigate drug overdoses. I don't know if they even asked anyone where he might have gotten the pills.

I remembered seeing Alex outside in the front yard curled up in a ball crying and mumbling. He was holding the St. Michael medal I had given John at our wedding for walking me down the isle. I asked Alex, "Could I have that back? I assure you I will give you something to remember John by. I don't blame you and I know John will watch over you. John loved you and thought you were the best drummer he's ever heard."

Teresa came to me and said, "You have to wait in the backyard until John's body is in the ambulance." I was so numb that I simply complied with those instructions. I feel even now that my numbness was a blessing for me. One of John's friends handed me a CD wallet with all John's original music in it. At that moment, I remembered one day several weeks earlier when I'd been driving him around so he wouldn't get arrested on the bench warrant, he'd told me he'd made up his funeral CD. I screamed at him for doing such a stupid thing, and didn't give him a chance to talk about the fact that he, too, knew he was going to die. He desperately wanted to talk to me about it but I was not strong enough to let him. He even sang about the fact that he knew he was going to die but would never kill himself. He made sure I found those words. He predicted his death in three songs, but I don't think anyone ever heard the songs until after he died.

As I was leaving John's house to go find my other children, John's dog, Guinness, was looking at me. He is the cutest English Bulldog that I have ever seen. I told David I needed to have him, even though just days before, we'd told John we wouldn't let Guinness live with us. Now I had to have him, for I could touch John through his dog. I became Guinness' person from that moment on.

By the time I arrived back at the house, my other sisters and their husbands were already there. Every time I saw someone new, I began crying again. I was dreading the pain of seeing Jamie and Michelle. When I came in the house, I collapsed on the couch and asked for a glass of wine. I'm pretty sure they just left the bottle close by.

I was worried about Jamie because she was pregnant and I didn't want the shock of John's death to put her into labor. She got to the house first and I could see she was going to be okay. It turned out to be Michelle who was in shock. I heard she was outside still in her truck and wouldn't come in. She just kept saying to herself, "Why is everyone saying John's dead? How could you know that?" I had to go out and tell her it was true. I don't remember the specifics but she still would not get out of the truck. She made it to the lawn outside my house and, after about an hour, came inside. The rest of the day became a blur.

I knew details of a funeral would be the next focus, but first and foremost, I wanted to keep peace in the family. Then I wanted John to know he was loved. It is customary for people to ask for donations to a charity instead of flowers. I had volunteered a lot of my time to charities and donated money all my life. For John, however, I wanted flowers. Lots of flowers. I also wanted him buried from the church. Even though I'd stopped going to church, I wanted a funeral Mass and nineteen white doves released at the graveside, one in honor of each year of his life.

In those early days, I remember the touch of my children became very important. When the girls would come over and hug me, it was as if I was touching them for the first time. The love exchanged through touch was so vibrant and, even though I was a touch therapist and keenly aware of the power of touch, this was as if it was in Technicolor. My sister Teresa said, "I'll coordinate everything for the funeral. All you have to do is tell me what you want." She is a "get the job done" kind of gal and I knew she would handle the details.

I went to bed, cried myself to sleep, and on Monday had to wake up for the first time after John died. That morning, I felt like I'd been punched in the stomach when the shock hit my consciousness. I wondered if it would ever go away. It was Monday and John Sr. would be coming in from Gettysburg as well as the families of my two out-of-town sisters. Other relatives were calling with their condolences and travel plans. This was the day of details – the priest, the cemetery plot, and the day of the Rosary, his burial, his clothes, his house, his guitars, his truck, his casket, and his cell phone. I must have asked and answered a million questions and made many difficult decisions. But the big questions remained unanswered: How did this happen? What was the last thing he did? Why, why, why? What did I do wrong?

At some point, Teresa got off the phone and said, "Regina, that was the coroner. He wants you to know John died peacefully, and did not kill himself." That didn't surprise me, because I never thought for one moment he'd committed suicide. The next thing I remember was someone coming in, saying, "John's father is outside." The moment seemed so surreal. We had given him life together and now we would bury him together. For a brief instant, nothing else existed except for the tears and the pain of that encounter. The years of tension before and after the divorce melted into the sorrow of that moment. We knew we would be kind, and treat each other with respect throughout these coming days. Nothing else was important enough to get upset over. Our son was dead and what else mattered but that we would say goodbye to him with love.

A priest, Father Joseph O' Brian, director of the St. Therese Center for HIV and AIDS where I had volunteered as a massage therapist for many years, would be able to say the funeral Mass at the Shrine of The Most Holy Redeemer Church across from the Luxor Hotel. I knew the power of this Sacrament for helping the soul pass through the stages of ascension into the higher levels of light. Although I do not agree with what most religions do, I am aware of the sacredness of the Holy Sacraments, Mass and Holy Communion being two of the most powerful. I was thrilled that I could have a funeral Mass said for John. Friday was the first day available at the church and I took it.

Wednesday was a private viewing for immediate family only, so no one but the family knew about it. I was glad I could have some time with my son before all of his and our friends and business associates would be there. I was exceptionally frightened about seeing his body for the first time. Sheer panic took over. In my heart, I thought I might die from sadness by just looking at him. This was more frightening for me than anything I could imagine. I have never been afraid of anything more than one of my children dying and now I had to face that one of them actually had. This was the thing I had dreaded and tried so hard to prevent. Had the warning that this could have happen been a blessing or a curse for me? What if it was a self-fulfilling prophecy? Could I have brought this upon him because I believed the original prediction?

The ride to the funeral home was like going to my own execution, with everything in extra slow motion. John was in the largest chapel, so even the walk to his coffin took forever. David and I arrived early in case I went completely nuts and he had to get me out of there. Finally I was beside the coffin and getting ready to kneel before it. I was calm and still breathing. Even in death, John was beautiful and I loved him so. I wondered how it would it feel to touch my child's cold hand. Would I die then? I felt he was still there. My eyes began to play trick on me, for I saw his eyelids move. I felt he was communicating with me already and that he would never stop.

There were only two members of my family I could even mention this to. My daughter Michelle and my niece Jen ... and they both had the exact same feeling. We knew everyone else would think we were crazy, so we just spoke about these things when we were alone.

On Thursday morning, the day of the public viewing and the Rosary, I was supposed to have been in the advanced training of Steve Rother's Spiritual Psychology class. Steve was going to do the channel at the retreat house in Mt. Charleston, and invited me to get the Group's perspective on John's death. The channeling was early in the morning so we would still have plenty of time to get to the funeral parlor by one o'clock. I invited Dominique, Jack and Brian, another close friend of John's, to come with David and me. On the way up to the retreat house, we started to listen to John's original music to choose which songs to play at the service that night. There were hundreds of songs to sort through. I knew Jen and John Sr. were going to sing. I had requested *Tears in Heaven* by Eric Clapton, the song he wrote after his five year old son passed away. Jamie had asked her father to sing that song at her sixteenth birthday party. The video we have of that song at the birthday party showed both John and his father through the whole song. John was only six then and was singing it along with his dad. I couldn't believe he would now sing it at his son's funeral.

The channel was long and I didn't hear much because I only cared about what the Group had to say about John. Less than two weeks earlier, I'd been on the Virtual Light Broadcast saying that traditionally, Mother Mary came before a tragedy and here I was sitting next to the window with Mary's image in it waiting for the Group to talk about John's death. Steve Rother hadn't even known I had a son until he was told on Monday when I didn't attend the training. He knew absolutely nothing about John, which made his message more important to me. All of my psychic friends who had known of John's possible death knew everything about us, so to me, Steve's information was never more real. It is not that I ever doubt what my friends tell me, but this was pure and genuine spirit contact, with no prior knowledge. An hour had gone by since Steve began the channel and I knew it was almost over. Finally, Steve got up from his chair and walked over to all of us sitting on the window ledge. It was apparent that this was difficult for him, but the Group began speaking through Steve:

"We wish to speak for a moment to the family that has come, for the family has lost a person, but not really. For the truth of the matter is, your son has left through a portal. You have a picture of it." (I had taken a photo of the weird cloud over John's house the morning he died. It looked like a huge funnel and lasted all day, without moving. Even the local evening news showed the unusual cloud on TV that night. Steve did not know of that photo until after the channel.)

Through Steve, the Group pointed to the window with Mary's image and continued, "You have the Mother who came herself to prepare you for what was about to happen. And what we wish to tell you about is the 'grand gift' he gave. The truth is that, even though it seemed he had a very difficult life, and even though it seemed he had great trouble in his life, it was through those difficulties he was able to pass on tremendous gifts to other people. To see himself in ways he could not otherwise. He is around you a tremendous amount, but he is not around you with sadness. He is around you with joy. And he's okay." (Steve's voice trembled as he spoke.) "He crossed over very quickly, effortlessly and painlessly. And he is HOME. He is laughing and he is enjoying the times that you are with him. For your intention to come together as a family is something he has always wanted to be a part of. He felt that he had difficulties sometimes even doing that. You have created the space for him to complete his life, and he just wants to say thank you."

I asked Steve to talk about whether a soul has many opportunities to leave. The Group replied, "When a soul comes in, you have a planning stage – the first stage of life. You sit down with all the potential people, and even though some may be on earth, you bring in their higher selves and they sit at the table with you, and you say, 'Will you be mom?' and, 'Will you be dad?' and, 'Will you be Aunt Harriet?' and, 'Will you be my first love in high school who will break my heart?'

You set all the opportunities up, and then you choose mom and dad, and you actually try to get them together in exactly the right time, and you're whispering in their ear, 'Aren't you feeling wonderful, and don't you love each other, and don't you want to go to bed together so you can have me nine months later under a certain sign.'

We tell you, those things you know as astrology are real. They are very important because you actually want to come in and be born under certain attributes. Not only are the astrological signs important, but also the birth order is important. For many people want to come in as the youngest, or the middle child, or the oldest, for that helps you fulfill your own life lesson you set up for yourself. Likewise, the time you leave also has imprints and cosmic events around it that help you acclimate when you go HOME. That helps you take those life experiences and acclimate them better. So there are windows of opportunity.

Your son had three phantom deaths, and this was his fourth. There were three opportunities for him to leave. He chose to stay. Had he been a coward, he could have taken the first one out. He was a very courageous man and you should be very proud of him. The reality is, HE DID HIS WORK. He did not stay around to enjoy, for he had difficulties with that part of this human experience. He had difficulties understanding what it was, and in a life lesson of "Being," you constantly feel incomplete and always want to add something to you, in some way to make you whole. That was very challenging for him. HE DID HIS WORK."

I asked, "Could he have stayed longer or was this the one he had to take?" The Group continued, "When you have a phantom death, there are three buttons you can push. It is a window, an opportunity that you set up. The first button says, 'I'm tired, I'm frustrated, I want to go home, so get me out of here as quickly as possible.' The second button says, 'I'm going to stay, and I'm going to move only into my passion, and I am going to do the things I came here to do and nothing more, and I'm really going to shine from this moment on.' And the third button says, 'I'll make my mind up later.'

What happened with your son is he pushed that third button three times; the fourth time, there are only two buttons. The challenge is about moving into what he came to do was the fact that he was new at this Mastery level of "Being."[1]

And he literally chose to share his gifts of what you would call negative, what has been known as failure, because with every negative, there is a positive. And by doing what he did, he affected more lives than he could have the other way around and that was his choice on the fourth time. And we know you are very proud of him."

I agreed, "I'm very proud of him. And his music is so beautiful, and we have a hard drive full of three years of him making the most beautiful music in his room. Much of the time he made it all by himself, or with a few of his beautiful friends, and it's so gorgeous. I think he will become famous just from what he did in his room."

The Group replied, "The truth of the matter is he's already famous. They have been waiting for him to return home for he had a very important job to do. He was greeted with open arms, and brought home to a hero's welcome." I said, "I know. I know he was."

The Group then said, "Espavo," which is their standard way of ending their channels. It's an ancient word that translates to: "Thank you for taking back your power."

---

[1] This is a reference to one of the 12 Life Lessons the Group talks about. The lesson of Being involves coming to see your own wholeness and inner beauty. Those in the throes of this lesson may look outside of themselves for whatever they think will complete them, which often leads to addictive behaviors.

Every word of the channel felt true to me. I was never a big believer in astrology and, of course, didn't want to be after the first time I had John's chart done. But now I felt there was a real basis in it. Steve accessed all of those exit points that Michele Avanti had told me about so many years ago. Other mediums would see John as a famous musician so I always focused on that and let John hear those parts of a reading.

My belief in John's talent was very strong. His father was once asked by Bruce Springsteen to be his lead guitarist and turned him down. I always told John he came to finish what his father didn't do and change the world through his songwriting.

On John's 17th birthday, the entire family and half the neighborhood went to Laguna Beach to celebrate (a family tradition). One of the local shops sold portraits painted by an artist who only did portraits of famous musicians and presidents. We had a painting of John done by this artist as a surprise. We arranged for him to "accidentally" find his own portrait hanging on the wall in the store. (John already had a painting by this famous artist of Bob Marley and he loved it.) We had that same portrait enlarged on cardboard the day of his funeral so his friends and family could write their final goodbyes in gold and silver ink on it.

John's energy was supporting me as I began a long day at the mortuary. It was around the corner from my house so I knew I could go home if I needed to. The viewing began at 1 p.m., and the Rosary wasn't until 6 p.m. When we came home from the channeling to freshen up for the long day ahead, I set up a full bar including ice and glasses in the trunk of my car.

In the chapel, it was standing room only. Even that huge room could not contain all the flower arrangements so they overflowed into the long hallway leading to the chapel. The song *Calling all Angels* started the services. I chose that song because it's the theme song to the movie *Pay It Forward*. I felt John had lived his life that way. The highlight was a five-song concert by his father. *Tears in Heaven* was the first song that I personally requested, and to my surprise, he had others planned with the words being changed in just the right places.

During the song *Yesterday* by the Beatles, when his father sang the words, "I said something wrong, now I long for yesterday," it was a "tear your heart out" moment. Everyone knew of the turbulent and verbally violent nature of their relationship, and I saw it as a public apology to John from his father. We all pretty much lost it right there. My body felt as if an earthquake of energy was running through it.

The final song was *Knocking on Heaven's Door*, a song John and his father played together all the time, and I motioned for everyone to get up and hold hands. He changed a line in the song from "Mama, take this badge off of me," to "Mama, put my guitars in the ground, I don't need them anymore."

All of John's guitars and artwork of his musical heroes were on display near the coffin, which was a fitting farewell and I was very pleased. Although I didn't cry during any of the public events, I sobbed throughout the night, every night, holding David tight.

Friday morning arrived, and the plans were to say, "Goodbye" privately at the mortuary. I sang a joyful song in honor of my new relationship with my son, for I knew in my heart this was the beginning of a new spiritual bond between us. Not the end of our relationship but the beginning of a new one. The song I sang in honor of this was called *It's a Joy to Get to Know You*. I then put a huge crystal he had given me in his coffin. I felt I could call his spirit in with the crystal acting like an antenna to his spirit. I would use this crystal as an etheric link. If crystals worked in computers and cell phones, I saw no reason why they wouldn't work across the veil. I knew our relationship was going to be very strong, and he would guide me from the soul plane. Even in those earliest days, I never felt he was out of reach.

More flowers and people arrived at the church and the Mass began. Teresa was to give the eulogy and you could hear a pin drop as she walked to the pulpit of the Shrine of The Most Holy Redeemer. Teresa was used to public speaking and this was to be a moment when time stood still. We were wondering if she could pull this off without breaking down. She began:

We've all seen pictures of our Little John these last few days. The beautiful collage that Eliana made. The amazing book that John's mother created for his 18th birthday. There's one picture of him that I carry with me every day ... even though it doesn't exist as a photograph. It only exists as a very vivid picture in my mind every time I think of him, and it always has. And I'd like to start today by sharing that with you.

In January of 1992, John was five years old, almost six. And my Kerry, who has been John's constant friend since before the day he was born was eight. John's cousin Beth was getting married in Dublin Ohio, and we all flew in for the wedding. On the morning of the wedding, Kerry and I were getting ready and a little knock came on the door of our hotel room and of course, who else would it be but Little John.

There he was in his little suit and tie, so adorable, and Kerry in her dress, so cute. And he stood there in his little John way of standing – kind of shrugging his shoulders – you know what I mean. And he and Kerry leaned up against a chair and John put his hand in his pocket and pulled out a roll of Lifesavers, just like in the old commercial. And he said,

"Kerry, want a Lifesaver?"

It was so cute. And so John. What kind of five-year-old boy gives away his candy?

Our John did.

That's the picture I'll always have because I'll never lose it because it doesn't exist on paper or in an electronic file. It only exists in my mind and my heart.

We all have those pictures of John that only exist in our minds and hearts.

John the generous. John the kind. John the giver. John who was such a family guy. He loved his mother and father and sisters and nephews and grandparents and aunts and uncles and cousins. His stepfather and mother and brother. John who loved to be around his family. John who loved his dogs and cat. John who just plain loved.

He loved his friends, too. His friends who are here with us today – Jack, Brian, Derek, Sharon, Jimmy, Jason and Kerry, who were his cousins and his friends. I can't name all of you but you're all here today.

You've come here today to pave the road for John's entry into the arms of our Heavenly Father. In the arms of the angels and saints and the Blessed Mother. At peace. In heaven there can only be peace for John and you know how he needed that peace.

I need to tell you about my John. And I say "my John" because he was so very special that he had a different relationship with each one of us. You all know what I'm talking about. You all had that special thing, whatever it was, that you loved to do with John. You all had those moments, those times when you thought of him. You all had that song. That one song or lots of songs that were special to just you and John.

But we all had different songs. I had a ton of 'em. I loved to pick out music that I didn't think he'd ever heard and give it to him. When he had his knee surgery, I went out to get him a couple of CDs. I wanted some classic Blue Grass and Blues for him. Some Chet Atkins. Some Muddy Waters. I thought I'd buy him 3 or 4 CDs. I think I ended up getting him about 20 because I kept seeing things I wanted him to have. I couldn't stop because I wanted him to have everything. Because I loved him so much. Just like all of us.

And for a young man, a boy, he was so open to learning any kind of music he could possibly get his hands on. I loved giving him that music. And he loved getting it. And I loved that he loved that. And so on. And so on. It was a constant exchange of loving and giving. A constant exchange of loving and giving. That's what we all had with John. It took a different form for each and every one of us, no doubt. But it was a constant exchange of loving and giving.

Each and every one of us here is grieving today. The loss of our friend, our nephew, our cousin, our grandson, our brother, our son. Your son.

And each and every one of us will carry that grief and experience that grief in as different and unique way as we experienced his life. His death is as personal to each of us as his life was.

As I've talked to you all these last days – all of you – as we've talked about how sad we are and how this can't possibly be happening ... and how much we loved John. I've learned that one person really can change the world.

John changed all of our worlds by being here. He changed them in a different way for each of us but there is absolutely no doubt. I know my world would have been much different if he'd never been here.

There's also no doubt each of our worlds will be changed forever because he's not here with us anymore. Our traditions with John. The J and R parties. The Laguna trips. Daily work at J and R. Gettysburg. Jamming with the boys. His nephew's birthdays. Breakfast. Lunch. Dinner. Family fights. Thanksgiving. My absolute favorite with John, Christmas Day at my house.

John's compassion for others – for each one of us and for people he never knew – for the children he hugged at Christmas and Valentine's Day at the Clark County Oasis Project. For the people he's touched with a rare and beautiful smile. And for the countless thousands who may never hear his music.

His music. It's hard for me to even talk about that because that was my personal relationship with John, as I know it was for so many of you. Music brought us together. It brought our family together. It brought you friends together. The band. It connected John with everyone he came in contact with. Music is magic ... and John's music was so much more than that.

John wasn't just talented. When he played his music, he left this world of pain and hurt and suffering ... and God played through him. God played through him. You could see it when he played – he was totally somewhere else and the music was just coming through him and touching us in ways that were not of this world.

We have all suffered an unimaginable loss. Unthinkable. Unfair. Unfathomable. Yet today, undeniable.

John is not here with us. And we are devastated. We are so deeply, deeply sad. And we will soon be very angry ... and that's okay. It's okay to be angry at the loss of someone we loved so much. Someone who never knew, could never grasp, how much we loved him. He was so busy giving his love to us that he didn't know how to receive it. He didn't know. I want everyone here to know this, and please don't ever forget it. You are loved. You Are Loved.

You were loved by John. And you're loved by God because you're his child. We're all his children and we are loved. Kerry, Matthew, Amy, Jen, DJ, Nick, you're loved by God. You must know this. All of John's friends. You must know this.

John was too sensitive for this world. Too giving. Too kind. Too good.

Our Heavenly Father knew it was time to relieve him of his pain. Our Heavenly Father knew that John so readily accepted other people's pain, so readily gave his love but he was unable to receive it. We all must honor John by learning to receive.

And we all ask ourselves today – and since last Sunday – what more could I have done? What one thing that I could have done might have saved him?.

Regina told us in her letter to us that we are not to feel any guilt at this tragic moment. She told us that the ultimate tragedy would be for us not to love ourselves in spite of John's departure from our world.

No one is to blame. No one. We all loved John.

You all need to know that John died very peacefully. His breath became so shallow that his body was not pumping enough blood into his heart ... and he slowly and peacefully went into the arms of our loving God.

This harsh world was not a place for a soul as gentle and loving as our John. God gave him to us as a gift to change our worlds for 19 years and to change our worlds again by knowing what it is to lose something beautiful ... and appreciate it more while we have it.

And so John is now comfortably and peacefully with our savior the Lord Jesus Christ, his loving Father, the creator of the world, the Holy Spirit and the Blessed Mother.

And we can celebrate because he is wrapped in warmth and light and love. And all the love he gave us is now surrounding him a thousand times. Please know that for certain and take comfort in that.

We cannot go back in time. But we can go forward in time. We can glorify John's life by cherishing our own. We can glorify John's life by loving each other. We can glorify John's life by accepting love when it's offered to us. We can glorify John's life by finding those people who are suffering more than we are here today and offering help. By feeding the hungry. By clothing the poor. By giving when it's hard to give, by loving when it's hard to love, by living when it's hard to live.

Gandhi said, "Be the change you wish to see in the world." We can all be that change that John wished to see in this world. We can give. We can love. We can nourish the world around us. We can accept love when it's hard to accept.

Let our gift to John be that we commit today to change the world. We commit to change the circumstances that led to his leaving us. We commit to share his music. We commit to love one another as John loved us ... as God loves us. The greatest commandment is: "Love one another as I have loved you." We commit to love one another as the Lord Jesus Christ loves us. We commit to know that the Lord Jesus Christ died for us so that we might live and that we know that John lives forever with our Lord and with us.

> John's gift to you today is a single rose. As you leave today, please take a rose as a symbol of John's love for you.
> I know that John is in heaven. My prayer for all of us here today is that when we go home, when we're going to sleep tonight, that God the Father wraps us up in his loving arms and cradles us like babies. Like many of us cradled John. That He fills us with His love ... and that He comforts us. He will comfort us. God Bless us all.

Teresa was beautiful and everything she said was beautiful. She was escorted out of the church by a trusted friend Jim to catch her breath. The next part of the Mass was Holy Communion. Out of the 300 people in the church, there was probably only a handful that could, according to "Canon Law," legitimately receive Holy Communion at the service. David and I and my children were not part of that handful, but we were well aware that my ex-mother-in-law was. We were also aware that if the shock of John's death didn't kill her, the trauma of 200 of John's friends lining up for Holy Communion might.

How funny those were my dominant thoughts at this time. The judgment of others was still a haunting issue, even after years of using the Emotional Freedom Techniques.

We all drove to the cemetery and someone was kind enough to have wine on ice in my limo. It was already "five o'clock somewhere," but I didn't care if it wasn't. I was amazed at how many people and cars were going to make the cross-town trip on a Friday afternoon in the busy Las Vegas traffic.

When it became time to let the 19 white doves out of the cage, the sky was beautiful and they flew around the area, putting on what seemed like an endless show for us. One lone white dove sat on a wire long after all the others flew home. It was as if it was John watching everything, and this did not go unnoticed by anyone. Everyone commented on it.

I didn't stay behind. I walked straight to the limo and it led the way to Teresa's house for the "party." Never would the Irish end a funeral without a great big party. Most weddings cost less than this whole affair, a gift from Teresa.

David and I sat at the same table as John's dad and his wife, and to the outside world, we were the best of friends. All the photos taken that night show so many orbs that the pictures looked like they were filled with champagne bubbles. After we all ate, Jimmy, one of John's friends, called us all in to watch the film he'd made about John's life. He is a filmmaker by trade and had been gathering footage of all his friends for years. What he had put together in just five days was the work of a genius.

From the moment the movie ended, trips to the airport began for all the out-of-town relatives and it was over. Everyone's life just went back to normal. Everyone's except those who were permanently crushed. David and I, John Sr., Jamie, Michelle, Dominique, Jack. The void was greater for those who had daily contact with John, as is always the case.

Chapter Fifteen

The Shock Is Over; the Grief Begins

The Meaning of the Tear in the Tapestry

What do you do the day after you bury your child or spouse, get diagnosed with cancer, lose your job, find out your wife is cheating on you, accused of a crime you did not commit, get raped, lose a limb, get drafted into a war you don't want to fight, lose your ability to take care of your family, suddenly realize you're addicted to painkillers, told that your child has autism or never arrived at school, have a stroke or a heart attack, are put into a long term care facility when your family can no longer keep you around, get into a car accident after you had two glasses of wine, or realize you are losing your memory little-by-little each day, to name a few.

Each day you wake up, you feel as if you're in the middle of a swimming pool. You're out of your depth, can't swim and can barely see the sides. You panic and realize you're alone. It doesn't matter how many hands are trying to reach out and help you. These are the things you go through alone when you wake up in the morning and realize your trauma was not a dream. It was real. Your life has changed forever. You wonder if the pain of waking up will ever lessen. You wonder why you even wake up if it is true. It would be easier to never wake up again, but you do wake up again and again, only to realize you now must learn to swim to the edge of that pool or you'll sink into a depression from which you will never recover.

Each day, you decide if you'll learn to swim or just allow yourself to sink to the bottom and die. Days come and go, and yet you still wake up in the center of that pool and must decide again to try to swim or just give up? You ask yourself, what matters? What really matters? The answer to that question is going to determine if you swim or sink.

Something has to matter. If you cannot find something to matter, you may not find the determination to learn to swim again. The other option is to stay alive only out of the fear of dying, but that is not living. This is like the movie *The Night of the Living Dead*. You never engage again in life. You simply go through the mechanics of functioning as a human being. Other people do not notice that you're not really there anymore, because you can "act out life" very well. The true essence of you begins to disappear behind the walls of a fortress within, and you don't care.

If you're lucky, after any of these things, there will be people who are relying on you for something. It could be family, relatives or just friends. If you are needed, you will have a better chance to recover. If you have children who need you, or people at work who are counting on you, or a spouse depending on you, or even a dog to care for, this can help. *The only real difference will be if you can find a dream for your life that still pulls at your heartstrings. A dream that can light the pilot light again in your heart.*

These are the things that can get you to learn to swim through the first year of a life-changing event. Nothing is easy about the adjustment period to a life that will never be the same. The most important thing for me was to be and feel productive. I knew I could still make a difference. The biggest difference I could make in this human form was to radiate thoughts of love. Even if we cannot speak or move a muscle, we can make a difference by radiating thoughts of love. Many souls who come in and seemingly have nothing to live for are here to emit love just by being where they are. They are human love amplifiers.

We have much to learn from these highly vibrating beings of light. If your whole world falls apart and you just begin to think loving thoughts, your world will be a brighter place. It is possible to train your mind to repeat a highly vibrating thought hundreds of times per day to lift you up. Something as simple as "Glory to God in the Highest," or, "My Gaze is only on God," or the phase, "I Love You, Jesus."

This is not to be confused with stuffing emotions and living in denial. I read that many of the prisoners in Nazi Germany would raise their hands and bless the tormentors in the death camps. They figured out that this blessing they sent out lifted their own pain and suffering. The intention was only to send love to their executioners but they found the blessing ran through them as an added gift.

It is only about choice of focus. No one can take away the power to focus our thoughts. It is always better to process the nagging thoughts so you can be sure the negative thoughts are not festering in your physical body. Hurt feelings, thoughts of self-judgment and blame are sometimes the most difficult to process and it takes determination. Most of us would throw out the sour milk in the refrigerator if we noticed it. The concept is the same: Being vigilant of repetitive negative thoughts and taking full responsibility for them requires courage.

For me, discovering every detail of the time between the last time I saw John and the moment of his death became one thing for me to live for. Doing a documentary about the tools I know did help him became another. Spreading the word about these methods on the website became a third. I had things to live for. I had a husband I adore, beautiful children and grandchildren who I still wanted to love and touch, as well as a granddaughter on the way and tons of clients I know needed me.

These were the things that kept me from sinking. There were many, many days when even all these blessings weren't even close to being enough to help me want to live, but then there were days they were. The first six months were filled with grief and tears. I cried so much I had acid burns on my face. I forced myself to put activity into my life. I committed to drive my grandchildren to school each day just to be sure I would get out of bed. I dedicated the website to John and sent out the thank-you notes, but I tried to avoid holidays and birthdays, especially his. Even though I was staying active, the grief was always calling out for my attention. And I secretly wanted to be alone just to grieve.

The Fine and Tender Threads Become Clear

Putting the pieces together of the last night of John's life happened over a long period. We could never tell if what we heard was the truth so we just waited to see what would surface. From what I know now at this point, when John left me for the last time on Thursday, he was starting to detox and was feeling bad. He called his friend Brian and told him he thought he was going to slip. John told Brian about a dream he had where he and his whole family did oxy with him. John told Brian that he thought the dream meant he couldn't get off oxy. Brian begged John not to take the Oxycontin again because he had come so far in the three days.

I should have realized John was starting to slip when he cut the session short on Thursday. He went to see his good friend Sharon on Friday night to talk to her about helping him stay clean. I think he had already taken Oxycontin but I don't know for sure. Sharon and John decided to work together on staying clean and kicking his drug addiction. I have only one report about Friday and that was that he drank a lot that night and had fallen asleep on his balcony. Jack, his best friend and roommate, realized he'd stopped breathing and had to pour water on him to wake him up. Also, I know his head injury was worse than anyone realized, for it had affected his breathing.

Saturday morning, John had called me very upset after hearing that his family all thought he was using drugs, and ended our conversation by hanging up on me. He was also still upset with me for me sending my son-in-law Glen to his house the prior week to tell him to get any drugs out of the house because of a possible police raid. He did not want anyone to know of his struggle with addiction.

I know he took Sharon out to lunch at IHOP on Saturday and they continued their discussion about helping each other stay clean. He ordered pancakes and French toast. They knew Jack didn't want Sharon at the house but John was going to ask Jack one more time if Sharon could spend the night. John told her, "If Jack doesn't agree, then I'll pick you up Sunday morning and you can help me take my belongings to my mom's house. Then we can have dinner. She's making macaroni." Sharon was happy she was invited. They'd been especially close for over 14 years, and John told her, "No matter what happens, I want you to know I love you." When she got out of the car, he gave her a CD by a group called Atmosphere. The song,

If I were Santa Claus, on the CD was for her. I know he'd bought Zanex after his lunch with Sharon, and probably started taking them right away. He told the guy he bought them from, "I can't wait to get out of Vegas and join the Red Cross. I want to see what it's like to just help people."

He called his cousin Jason to come over to discuss the rental of the house and he confronted Jason about him telling the family John was addicted to drugs. Jason did not deny the accusation and John just dropped it. Many of John's friends, including Jack, were going to a concert that night. John stayed home to pack for the move back home Sunday morning. He called his friend Jimmy and asked him to come and get him. He told Jimmy, "If I don't get out of the house tonight, I'll die."

Jimmy didn't have transportation and John was already so wasted he couldn't drive. He called Sharon and pretty much told her the same thing, but she couldn't drive. It's interesting that John called the only two people he knew couldn't drive. Apparently, some of John's musician friends came over to jam on his last night in the house. During that jam session, Jack came home along with Alex. Jack knew he shouldn't have brought Alex but it was hard to leave him in the streets. Alex was always hoping for a place to sleep indoors as he was living on the street at the time. Alex didn't go inside but waited outside for John.

While they were jamming, John went to his truck to get his phone. He had spoken to Dominique several times that night, and she could sense he was on something and they'd fought over it. He denied taking anything but she could hear in his voice that he had. Since they were arguing, he wanted to talk in the truck so no one could hear him. When he went outside, Alex approached him and begged him to get him some oxy. John never went back into the house and abandoned the friends he was jamming with, leaving without even a goodbye or an explanation as to why he was leaving. The guys he was jamming with got pissed off that he had left them and they all just went home. John took $200 out of the bank and then charged another meal at IHOP. (I guess if I knew I was leaving the planet today I might consider two meals at IHOP.) According to Alex, John bought five oxy for him, and he immediately took one. John was complaining about the pain in his head, so Alex gave John one oxy. John told Alex, "Don't let me fall asleep because I'm having trouble breathing." They sat up and played guitars in the bedroom. At one point, Alex walked John around because he realized he might be in trouble from too many drugs. Then they played for a while longer and eventually fell asleep. When Alex woke up and saw John was blue, he knew immediately he was dead and had been dead for a while. Jack had already left the house to have breakfast with his mom, so Alex called Jack to tell him, "John's dead and I've called the police." That's when Jack and his mother came to my house with the news that would change my life.

Chapter Sixteen

Communications Across the Veil

In the past, the ability to have communication with loved ones who have crossed over was a concept held to be "wishful thinking" by the mourning relatives. Psychics and mediums were labels for individuals who claimed to have these mystical but "unreal" powers of being able to communicate with "the other side." In recent times, as science and life experiences surfaced about the possibility, the subject became intriguing and drew interest from the public, and has become an accepted concept. Some of the well-known TV psychics who can communicate across the veil have developed a huge following. Their profession is recognized as important and real.

John Edward hosted his own TV series – Crossing Over with John Edward – that began in the 1990s. In that series, he did psychic readings for live television audiences. There is a three-year waiting list to have a personal reading with him. He has written many books and seven were on the best-seller lists.

Sylvia Browne started her career of doing psychic readings in 1973 and has written 37 books. Seven of her most recent books have been best-sellers. She has made weekly appearances on the Montel Show for 16 years and does psychic readings with the audience. She does personal readings but they are booked months in advance. She has her own show at the Excalibur in Las Vegas, Nevada.

Two popular, Emmy Award winning, weekly TV shows – Medium and Ghost Whisperer – both portray the ability to communicate with others who have crossed over to the other side of the veil.

There is little doubt that this type of communication is coming to the forefront of our belief system. More and more information is becoming available about people's abilities to not only communicate but also to see and describe people who have crossed over. Both John Edward and Sylvia Browne have this ability.

I, too, have been getting communications from John that are later validated by actual happenings and events. I would like to share the experiences with you.

I read everything I could about communication from the other side of the veil, and I began receiving messages from John just a few days after he died – strong, direct communication with specific directions followed by validation that he really was in touch with me. Many people reported to me about miracles seemingly from John and dreams about him. Only two weeks after his death, I arranged for a session with my good friend Cheryl Johnson, a gifted medium, who had known John. I wasn't sure if he would be able to communicate yet, since he was still "the new kid on the block" up there, but I couldn't wait any longer. I had so many questions and I felt him around so much that I needed to know I wasn't losing my mind. I didn't know if I could actually have a conversation with him, but I was hoping I could and was excited about having a conversation with him. I was still too early in my grief to know how much fun we would have down the road working together and he didn't bother to clue me in. The session was incredible and proved to me there is no such thing as "dead." In fact, far from being my dead son, he is suddenly my "highly vibrating son." As always, Cheryl began with a prayer.

Cheryl: Mother Father God Friend, we thank you for blessing our gathering. We are open only to the light and your guidance, and we are very grateful. And so it is. John says that you knew right away that he didn't ...

Regina: Kill himself?

C: Yes.

R: Oh yeah, I knew right away, without a doubt he didn't kill himself.

C: Okay, all right, so what do you want to ask him, or do you want to just see what he has to say?

R: Let's see what he has to say.

C: Okay (we both laugh) you are aware of the song he wrote for you?

R: The one about Jesus?

C: Yes. And he wrote one to his dad?

R: Yes.

R: What does he want us to do with his music?

C: Cherish it. Just cherish them. It's very personal.

R: So he doesn't want us to try and make him famous?

C: Get the message out. It's not about getting famous; it's about people hearing the songs, remembering them and living them.

R: Is he going to be there when I cross over?

C: He's going to be there, he is supposed to greet you. I said, "supposed to," but he said, "Gets to," laughing.

R: Did he like his funeral?

C: He's pretty amazed at how many people showed up. He didn't know he had that effect.

R: Was he happy that Bill showed up?

C: A little surprised. I don't know why, but he is touching his heart.[1] He also likes his clothes. (This made me wonder about wearing clothes in heaven.)

R: What did he think about his father's songs?

C: Heartbreaking.

R: Right, they were heartbreaking.

R: When did he make the final decision?

C: He says, "I made the final decision on the other side right before the injury to my head, but (with emphasis) I didn't know on your side until just before." He shows himself as almost anesthetized, as if part of him goes over to the other side, so he's not fully present. He shows that from the time of the head injury, he wasn't here enough to do anything about it.

R: So he couldn't reverse the decision at that point?

C: NO (emphatically). The decision was made.

R: Has he met John Lennon yet? I had a vision of that last Thursday.

C: Yes, and Jimmy Hendrix. Oddly though he says Harry was first.

R: Harry Chapin?

---

[1] This was a reference to Bill, a hotel owner we did work for and a long time family friend who we all respected a great deal. John was always hurt that his father didn't introduce him to Bill when he had the chance. John felt his father was ashamed of him. He was standing right next to Michelle at a J & R Flooring Christmas party and his father only introduced Michelle. He was deeply hurt by that. He always brought it up when he was hurting. Also the fact that there were no pictures of him in his father's office hurt him. He would count how many there were of his stepbrother every time John Sr. added a new one. Because his stepbrother was in the service, his father kept adding photos of him in uniform and on the battlefield. Naturally everyone always asked how his "son" over in Iraq was doing. John could never get over those two things, so I made a point of making sure Bill knew John had passed away. I wanted to introduce him myself. I think John understood that and that's why he touched his heart.)

C: He wants you to know he was not talking to Harry about the music so much as the messages in the music.

R: Wow![2]

C: That might explain as to why Harry came first and he is just fascinated.

R: Is it possible for anyone to hurt him on that side?

C: No.

R: Was he mad at me when he left?

C: NO (emphatically).

R: Well, in the last conversation we had, he was.

C: It's a pattern. He's showing this as a repeating pattern. If he had woken up the next morning, you guys would have been fine again, same as always. Was he mad at you when he crossed over? No, he wasn't even aware when he crossed over, and he wasn't mad when he was talking to Dominique on the phone, because this is something you and he had done over and over again. He said he'd never admit it on this side but he'll admit it now. He says you and he argued because you talked about who he really is. This was an ongoing argument between the two of you and he didn't really want to see it.

R: You mean because I believed in him and he didn't?

C: You kept showing him something true but he declared it false, yet he couldn't win. There was no way he could disprove it so he would just get mad, and you were right.

R: Is there anything he wants me to do, pay attention to?

C: He's singing to you now. He says lyrics are coming through to you and it's just a song for you. I don't know if it's part of a healing. I can literally see music. Like when the angels show music. I can see that coming down and it's beautiful.

---

2 This made so much sense to me because every time we would go on an appointment together, we would have to agree on the music. He would say every time we got into the car, "Is Harry in the car?" Harry was the number one favorite of my CD collection that he always wanted to hear.

R: My ears are throbbing. Does he meet Mary?

C: Yes, but Mary didn't look like what he expected.

C: He shows me a picture of Mary and it's very traditional. He says she doesn't look like that.

R: What does she look like?

C: He says, "She's the most beautiful being I have ever seen. There was a lot of light. I was stunned with the energy."

R: Did she put her arms around him?

C: Yes. He says, "Mary seemed huge, when actually she's a tiny person, but the energy was overwhelming."

R: Oh, wow.

C: He says, "I cried. I actually cried. I cried because somebody loved me so much."

R: The Group said Mary came to the window to prepare me for his passing. Does he know that?

C: He didn't know that when he was alive, just as you didn't know. He does now, but he didn't then. You know that Mary wasn't any more clear on that she was preparing you for John's death because the decision had been made, right?

R: Right.

C: The decision was that firm. He went out on a "win." It was very important in this lifetime that he goes out on a win, which is why the decision was so firm.

R: And going out on a win means he pulled the family back together?

C: That he pulled himself back together. Within the last year, he shows himself coming out of quicksand.

R: Right.

C: He says, "And because of that, I'm a win, I'm doing it, I'm breaking the pattern, time to go." By the way, he says, "Thank you. I don't feel like I thanked you enough."

R: Is there anything in my life he wants me to do for him before I cross over?

C: For him, NO.

R: For the world?

C: You are going to do that anyway. He wants you to open more to the joy. Remember, it's like a joyride, a thrill ride. He is showing the core, right here. He wants you to open more for the joy for yourself, as well as for others. He says it's like him expressing through you.

R: Okay. Is he going to be able to continue communicating with me?

C: He says don't worry about him communicating with you. That won't be a problem.

R: I hear him more while I'm awake.

C: That is one of the projects he set for himself. Your work. You know he is fascinated with it. You used to tell him a little bit about it but it went right over his head. On the other side, he actually gets to see the movement of the energy within your clients. It's almost like a science fiction movie. Some of the things go back to past lives, going to other dimensions, and into the future.

R: Right.

C: He's fascinated.

R: Did he cause that huge lawsuit to go into mediation?

C: He assisted. Thank you, yes. By the way, he thinks they're a bunch of fricking a**holes.

R: The prosecutors? Well, I love him!

C: And he loves you, too! Are you aware he was born to you to assist him to live long enough to get the WIN?

R: No.

C: He's talking about coming into this lifetime to have to clean up this pattern.

R: Really.

C: Yes. He says, "The reason I was born to you is your extreme faith, even when I was dragging myself down." He shows you with him in a chokehold, holding him up, like there's no way in heaven or hell you're going to let him go down. And what happened is, you bought enough time for him to start bringing himself out.

R: So he was mastering the life lesson of Being. When he comes back, will he walk in mastery of the life lesson of Being?

C: He says, "I think I would say 'baby' mastery." He's looking as if to say, "Not there yet." But an awful lot of chains were thrown off in this lifetime. That's why you brought him in.

R: I'm happy to have assisted him. It's my honor.

C: He is grateful and hugging you. He says, "That's exactly what you would say."

I was ecstatic with the session after it was over. I'd had so many questions and John had answered every one of them. There were so many things in his answers that Cheryl could not have known about, even though she had known him personally, such as John's love of Harry Chapin's music. She did only one reading with him, but John always came up when I had a reading with her. I couldn't wait to share this reading with everyone who would be interested. I got up at three a.m. to transcribe the tape and, while I was typing, I heard some unusual music somewhere in the house. It wasn't always there; it would come and go. I got up several times to see if I'd left something on, like the Cable TV's Soundscape channel or a CD playing in the bedroom. Finally, I realized it was on the actual tape I was playing, stopping and starting it in order to transcribe the words on the computer.

The music started when I was typing: "He's singing to you." It finally dawned on me the sound was actually on the tape and coming from John. (That he managed to impose his vibration on the tape amazed me.) The music was so beautiful I could hardly believe it. It was the most beautiful sound I'd ever heard, something like whale song and yet not exactly. Each time I had someone listen to it, I could see the shock on their face as they heard it. It was obvious they had never heard anything like it, either.

It was becoming apparent that John was going to prove to me that there is no such thing as "death." He sent sound through one other time but it was not as loud or clear. I listened very carefully each time I had a session with Cheryl to see if he sent anything else on the tapes. I even left his computer on "record" at night to see if he would send something to me that way, but no sounds ever came through the computer so I stopped. My web site has this audio file available to listen to.

John's first communication directly with me took place in the middle of the night. I was suddenly wide-awake about three in the morning. We probably have all have had that wonderful feeling when you have the alarm set for 5 a.m., wake up at 3 a.m. and know you are not going to fall back asleep until 4:45 a.m. I thought I heard John tell me to send an email to Susan, my friend who makes the jewelry. I began to talk to him out loud asking, "Why do I have to send an e-mail at three in the morning?" He said something like, "Because I say so. Ha, Ha."

I could hear the humor in his voice, I think coming from his funny side, meaning, "Like now you have to listen to me." I didn't even believe I was hearing him, but I sent the e-mail anyway, telling her: "I'm sure everything is going to be fine. I'm sure Teresa will find a way to make it better." (This was a reference to a lawsuit involving the company owned by her father.) I never had the guts to say it was John who made me write the e-mail.

Was all of this in my imagination? I wasn't hearing this with my ears but in my mind. I had completely forgotten that Susan used to baby sit John for me. She and I have always had a spiritual connection, and she was always interested in what I was learning. For example, after I became a Reiki Master, Susan did also. If I learned something new, I always called her to share it with her. If I were teaching a class, she would be there. We had more of a "mother/daughter thing" as she is about the same age as my daughters. We also marveled at the fact that my sister was an intricate part of her company's strategy for solving their problems.

The only thing on my mind at that moment was that my son was asking me to make a fool out of myself and tell Susan something that made no sense. There was no reason at that point to believe there would be a change in the lawsuit but I had stopped worrying whether people thought I was "crazy." I figured I could get away with "being crazy" for at least the first year after John died.

Good validation came the next day around 3 p.m., when Susan's father was informed that the lawsuit was going into arbitration, which was a giant blessing for all of them!

Another validation I received came on the next day when I was looking for all the videos of family functions I'd taken through the years. I was going to watch every last one to see how much footage I had of John. We had just remodeled the house and all the videos were misplaced. David and I searched everywhere but couldn't find them. I was filled with panic that during the remodeling, I might have inadvertently tossed out all the videos of John's life. I went over to his piano where I kept a crystal he had given me and spoke to it as though John was there. I demanded, "Tell me where the videos are." Then, on a hunch, I went over to a wicker chest in the front room and opened it. All the videos were safely stored there although I had no memory of putting them there, so I sent John a silent "thank you." On top of the videos was one photograph. It was of my son and Susan's father, Paul, when John was about ten. In the photo, John was behind her father looking over him with a smile. John told me, "Take the photo to Susan's dad." That's all he told me at the time.

Since I used to do a great deal of business with Susan's father, I was well aware that this would seem really weird to him. We had a long relationship and he had been at all the funeral service for John, but I still felt really uncomfortable taking him a picture of my son. I drove to his office and sat down in his office while he finished a call. Once he'd hung up the phone, I thanked him for the flowers he had sent and for coming to the services. I then gave him the photo and just blurted out, "John is telling me to tell you that the lawsuit will be over by your birthday and settled in your favor."

I really didn't want to tell him I was talking to dead people but John had insisted. If John had told me before I left the house that he was going to make me say that, I would not even have gone. He looked at me very strangely. I had expected him to thank me and then tell my sister Teresa who consults for him that I had lost my mind. Instead, what he then said surprised me. He told me, "I've just gotten off the phone with the arbitrator, and the arbitration is set for the day before my birthday."

That was enough for me to start trusting I was hearing John. As it turned out, the arbitration was settled by his birthday, and in his favor.

Holidays were always special to John but Christmas even more so. When I was driving home from Jamie's house after watching them open the presents, I remembered how John wanted all of his family to love each other and get along. After the divorce, as in many families, trying to fit all sides of every family in at Christmas took great planning, as our family was rich with traditions. John was particularly fond of one member of my ex-husband's family. Known to all as "Uncle Tony," he looked like Telly Sevalis in *Kojak*, and had habits that drove my ex-husband's family crazy. John loved him and would invite him to all of the functions on my side of the family. However, when he invited him to functions on his father's side, they would all get angry with John, who could not accept that his father's family discarded Uncle Tony. At one of the last Christmas dinners before he died, John caused a huge fuss on Christmas Eve and was yelled at by his grandfather for inviting Uncle Tony to his Dad's house for Christmas dinner, so he left the dinner and came home. John had his principles and hurting Uncle Tony was not acceptable to him. I was SO proud when he did that. This was a great memory and reminded me that John's love of others was sacred to him and he wouldn't bend his principles.

When we arrived home on the first Christmas after John died, we found out that Uncle Tony had passed away at three that afternoon. My response was, "Wow!! John got to spend Christmas Dinner with Uncle Tony after all." I now knew that John wasn't alone at Christmas. I never told Uncle Tony about John's death because his own health was failing. He had no children and was so fond of John that I knew he would take the news of his death really hard.

About two weeks after Christmas, I received a frantic call from Vickie, the woman who had been taking care of Tony. He'd lived in her home, and that's where he'd died. She received a call from her ex-husband who was in Big Bear California for the holidays. They lost a daughter called Sara, and she often appeared to them over the years. Vickie's ex called Vicky to say he'd had a strange visitation from their daughter. "Sara wanted you to know that Tony had Christmas dinner with John. I have no clue what this message means but I'm delivering it exactly as I heard Sara say it." Vicki's ex-husband didn't know that Tony passed away because his cell phone didn't have coverage in the mountains. Vickie and I both knew the meaning of this simple message and were both overwhelmed.

Chapter Seventeen

Grief Grows Like a Weeping Willow

I ran into a friend who told me of some terrible verbal abuse John had experienced at the luncheon the day before my wedding. John Sr. was sitting next to him at the table with the entire family in the restaurant after the Holy Communion for my grandson. About fifty people in all attended the luncheon. He described in great detail what his father and grandfather said to him during that meal. His words as best I can recall were, "I've never heard anyone treated with such brutality." My friend tried to console John by putting his hand on his shoulder but John just pushed it away, got up and left the table. I recall John coming over to me and saying that he wanted nothing to do with his dad again. He spoke those words often after a conversation with his dad, so I didn't pay close attention to him and just tried to ease his pain. I was getting married the next day so I probably let it go without much effort. Encounters with his father were either wonderful or horrible. This one was particularly horrible, especially because it was in public in front of so many people. After I got home that day, I went into John's room and laid on his bed – the one he'd died on – and I cried in a way I had not ever done before. The agony of his abuse was so painful, even nine months after he died, that I wept from the depths of my soul. He had cried himself to sleep in this bed so many times and the pain was unbearable. Hearing about this abuse from his father made me realize how much John didn't tell me about his pain. I cannot tell how long I cried but, as I drifted off to sleep, I felt him touch the side of my face. Then he kissed my eyelids and said, "Mom, I love everyone you love, and I am watching out for them."

He could have just said, "Mom, I love you," but he didn't. His kiss healed my heart and in an instant made me realize he was working with me in my healing room. This actually brought me great joy. I could feel he was going to be watching over everyone I love, and I knew that also meant everyone I work with. Wow, that was something to ponder. I felt as if he was my partner and that we could do great things together.

It wasn't long after that; I was having another party on my boat with all my sisters. By this time, there were tons of orbs coming out in the photos from my camera and lots of unusual and interesting energy. I always "auto enhanced" my photos to see what was out of the ordinary.

This time so much energy was on the photos that I was really getting excited. I always looked several times just to be sure I viewed everything. To my surprise, a very clear image of John came through, watching over my sister who was recovering from a stroke. (See this photo on the back cover of the book). This was the second time an actual image of him had come onto a picture, and much clearer than the first. Needless to say, I was thrilled. What I didn't realize at the time was the extent to which he would communicate with me through my camera. At the time, I thought it was just a one-time gift from John but as time went on, I realized the camera would be his way of working with me in the healing room.

Can Grief Be an Addiction?

About a week before my nephew's wedding, I was again on the boat, alone and crying. The boat had become my sanctuary to grieve for John. The last time I held my son was at my wedding in May when we danced to the song: *You Are the Sunshine of My Life*. I was worried I would break down and cry when my nephew danced with his mom at his upcoming wedding, bringing back this memory of my last dance with John. I decided to think about the upcoming event and just cry it out so I would be fine and not cry at the wedding.

In fact, I was making myself sick over it, and was obsessed with the thought of breaking down at my nephew's wedding. Every chance I got, I'd go to the boat and play a song that would make me cry. On a gloomy day just before the wedding, I was on the boat crying and I heard John's voice as clear as day, saying very loudly, "WILL YOU JUST TAP." I heard this with my human ears and the sheer volume startled me.

Of course, I teach people to tap but never even thought of using it for my situation. I am the queen of denial but decided to give it a try. I began with, "I deeply and completely accept myself even if I am afraid I will cry it at the wedding when Diane dances with her son." Instantly the pain was gone and I was absolutely fine. What a surprise! That must mean this tapping works for me, too, I thought. What do you know? I will never stop being amazed at how much we humans love pain and suffering. I teach tapping every day and yet I can't even remember to do it for myself. Don't I feel like the drama queen now?

Of course, as the moment approached at the wedding, my daughters were hovering close by in case they needed to hide me, but I did great. I was amazed, grateful and thrilled as all of the other wedding guests applauded at seeing the "Mother and Son" dance.

When I was alone in the afternoons after a day of seeing clients, I would often think about John, put on a video of the funeral and just cry. One particular day, I had some filing to do in my office, so I decided to combine crying and mourning with filing. I poured a glass of wine and pulled out all the DVDs of John that brought on the tears, but not a single DVD would work. I began to get really frustrated as one DVD after another failed to play.

Finally, I got to the last DVD, which covered the last year of his life and it included a clip of a practice session with his sister for an audition for the Suncoast Casino and Hotel. They hated it when I filmed them and told me, "Don't you dare." I said fine and went upstairs. At the top of the stairs, I lay on the floor and filmed through the banister. I was sure I was well hidden but John saw me and yelled in his angry booming Italian voice, "TURN THE F***ING THING OFF," which I promptly did.

I put this last DVD into the computer and for no reason, it began playing at exactly the spot when he yelled: "TURN THE F***ING THING OFF." I restarted the DVD but the same thing happened. After the fourth time of the same command, I cracked up laughing. I realized John was controlling the computer and was telling me to turn it off. He didn't want me to watch anything that made me sad and was letting me know I was addicted to crying, mourning and grieving.

I understood instantly how we become addicted to a vibration of an emotion. Grief was like candy for me and I knew it, so this insight was the biggest "Aha" I'd had in a long time about a vibration. I realized we become addicted to such vibrations as blame, anger, sadness, fear and self-loathing. My addiction was grief and he was teaching me this through the computer. I put on some happy music and filed away. However I did finish the wine and did it in joy and not in sadness.

This realization helped me a great deal in my sessions with Emotional Freedom Techniques. "Even if I am addicted to blame, fear or whatever" was always added whenever I sensed the vibration was an actual addiction. Blame often pops up, especially when the program of being a victim is deeply embedded in the subconscious. For a quick five minute demonstration of exactly how this works, you can just go to my website and click on the bar that says, "Learn emotional tapping techniques."

Another Piece of the Tapestry

Experiencing grief and sudden loss was not only part of my journey but now affected Susan's family. She called me to discuss the death of her grandmother and how important it was for her to travel to New York for the funeral. On the plane trip home, she had a strange experience. She felt a loving message come to her from who she believed to be her grandmother. She knew it was a gift from the other side of the veil and that this being had great love for her. She assumed it was her grandmother since she was just at her funeral.

When she landed in Las Vegas, she found 13 phone messages from her family, telling her that her mother had tragically died while Susan had been traveling home from her grandmother's funeral. This seemed unusually traumatic to me. I was already close to Susan but this seemed to connect us even more.

Susan's mother also died of prescription drug abuse. She was prescribed "pain killers" in her mid- thirties and that began a downhill spiral for her. Until then, Susan's mother was a very responsible wife and mother, but her life began to unravel shortly after her introduction to these drugs. We had each other to discuss our grief and how crazy one can get while processing this kind of shock. "Death by overdose" was another thread connecting our families.

~ ~ ~

In September 2006, the first anniversary of John's death was rapidly approaching and I was beginning to get nervous. I knew I was not yet strong enough to do anything elaborate at the graveside, and that too much attention to the anniversary would cause me to wallow in sadness again. We decided to wait to have an organized function until what would have been John's twenty-first birthday, which was only a few months away. On October 1, David and I decided to celebrate John's life by going to see "LOVE" at the Mirage Hotel and Casino. This is a musical with only Beatles music and John was a huge Beatles fan.

On October 2, the anniversary of John's death, I ordered a "bleeding heart" flower arrangement and took it to the graveside when I went to the cemetery with David and Michelle. I also designed some pillowcases to commemorate John. His father had sung a song at the funeral with the words, "There are tears on the pillow where you slept, and you took my heart when you left." I had those words and a heart embroidered in red on gold pillowcases. I put my pillowcase on the actual pillow John died on, and gave others as gifts to everyone I knew was still really hurting. The anniversary was over and I knew I would breathe easier with that behind us. I went to bed looking forward to year two being much better.

Chapter Eighteen

Death Knocks Again

Early the next morning of October 3, 2006, one year after my son died, I noticed David getting out of bed and I glanced at the clock. It was only 4 a.m., which meant I had another hour in my warm comfortable bed. I turned over and snuggled myself under the covers, happy to know I could drift off one more time before 5 a.m. to drive my grandchildren to school.

Suddenly, I heard John say, "Go downstairs now!" I said out loud, "I know you're my imagination, and I'm not getting up!" John repeated, "NOW!" which I heard with my human ears, so loud and clear it made me jump. I knew this could not be good, so I leaped out of bed and found David leaning over the kitchen counter looking really awful. He thought it was indigestion so I gave him some coconut milk, which had always been an instant fix. I was up so I made my coffee knowing I would not be going back to bed.

His indigestion didn't get any better so I gave him applesauce and bread, and then my tuning forks. Finally, he said, "Hon, get me to the hospital."

That trip happened in slow motion. David got into the car without his shoes. I, being in total denial said, "You need your shoes." David replied, "I won't be needing them, hon." I said, "Oh YES, you will." It was my way of not allowing this to be a heart attack. I wasted a minute by getting his shoes. Although I am a normally slow driver, it was as though the car couldn't go faster than five miles an hour. Part of me knew my life was about to change again.

David couldn't get out of the car so I pulled up to the emergency door and pounded on it for help. They came right away and put David in a wheelchair. They told me to park the car and fill out the forms. Before I finished the paperwork, the doctor came out of the emergency room and told me, "Prepare for the worst. David is having a very bad heart attack. We're calling in the cath lab (I didn't know what that was) but I'm not giving you any good news."

By 9 a.m., they had determined that all five arteries were blocked and they needed to do a five-way bypass. The medicine they gave him to stop the heart attack did not work and he was still having a heart attack. The surgeon told me, "There are other complications, too. Go in and talk with David for a moment while I get ready to operate."

What do you say in one minute to someone you love when it could be the last thing you will ever say? This man held me up through ten years of struggle including John's death, and now he was facing his own. I could see he was afraid and I was paralyzed by my own fear. I was so frozen in panic that I couldn't even say, "You'll be okay, hon." Instead, I managed to ask him for his son's phone number as if it was just an ordinary question. He asked me if he had to have the surgery. I told him "Yes" and he felt I was right, even though we both knew his odds weren't good. Suddenly, it was time for him to go. I kissed him goodbye and said, "I love you, I'll be right here," just as I do every day. Then they rolled him away and he was gone.

My daughters came to sit with me while David was in surgery. I sat in a chair that was not facing the doors of the operating room that the doctor would come out of to talk to me. I knew that I would know the outcome from just the look on his face. Again I was terrified. Jamie has the best sense of humor (dry and irreverent) and would say the funniest things to help lighten me up. After I would laugh I could get a well-needed breath.

After the surgery, David was fighting for his life day after day, and getting him off the respirator was always a concern. One day, about a week after the operation, I could see something had gone terrible wrong when they started looking at the kidney function. When I leaned over to check something under the sheet, I could feel that David was all wet and there was blood on the sheet. I knew enough to know that this was really critical. This really scared me and for the first time, hope was gone. I left the hospital screaming at God, "IF I'M SUPPOSED TO STAY POSITIVE, THEN YOU'D BETTER DO SOMETHING RIGHT AWAY TO HELP ME BELIEVE DAVID CAN SURVIVE!"

I was literally screaming at God in the parking lot as I walked to my car. For good measure, I added, "AND ANOTHER THING. I THINK IT'S IN ESPECIALLY BAD TASTE TO GIVE DAVID A HEART ATTACK JUST HOURS AFTER HE LEFT JOHN'S GRAVE!"

We had purchased the two plots to the right of John's, so technically David was standing on his own grave when we brought the flowers to the grave on John's anniversary. I asked God, "DO YOU HAVE A WARPED SENSE OF HUMOR OR WHAT? AND ARE YOU HAVING FUN SCREWING WITH ME?"

I was yelling and crying but I do remember there was no one around. I didn't want to make a fool of myself in public. I stayed at the hospital practically round the clock, keeping in touch with the world through email. I would go home at 5 a.m. when they asked me to leave so he could have his bath. I told everyone not to call me, no matter what, because I would not leave David's side to answer the phone. Just as I finished scolding God again for what seemed cruel and unusual punishment, the phone rang. It was Susan. "I know we're not supposed to call but I was instructed to. I was doing remote Reiki on David and Jesus came in and told me to stop. Jesus told me, 'Tell Regina that David is going to be fine.'" There was much more, but that was the general message.

At this point I was not sure if I believed anything. I honestly believed I would be asked to sign a DNR (Do Not Resuscitate order) when I returned. We had discussed this in length before making our living wills, and I know David would not want to be kept alive if it was hopeless. I was crying out of control and went home, poured myself a glass of wine and went to the boat. It was really early in the day to be drinking, but I didn't care. I hadn't eaten or slept in days and was at the end of my rope. I needed a miracle.

Susan had just given it to me, yet I didn't believe it. These things don't happen. In real life, you don't scream at God and then get a phone call with a message from Jesus answering your prayers just like that. Was that just another cruel joke or was David really going to recover?

After my pity party ended about 30 minutes later, I decided to go back to the hospital and face the music ... whatever that may look like. When I returned to the ICU, David's kidneys were fine. Apparently, there had been a kink in the catheter line and that's what was causing the problem. The line ruptured, which is why David was wet. If the line hadn't ruptured, the fluid would have backed up and caused septic shock or could even have ruptured his bladder.

This had been a close call, hence the apparent miracle I needed to believe David would come home to me. It gave me validation to believe that what Susan said was true. Jesus intervened for us. I even felt healed, and my strength to face the long journey ahead was renewed. It is astounding that Susan's father calmed me down when I thought John Sr. was going to die, and now, 25 years later, Susan does the exact same thing. If we could only see how the thin threads of our life's tapestry connect us with each other, life would be a lot less confusing.

A week later, David was still on the respirator and still not doing well enough to breathe on his own. There was talk of putting him in a special hospital for patients who cannot get off the respirator. To him, this would be a fate worse than death (literally). Every day was a roller coaster ride. We finally got him off the respirator (with the help of Charmaine Lee and Jon Olson, my friends and great healers) and I took him home. David's family never left us alone until we were okay. His son and brothers took turns and stayed at the hospital with him and handled all of our needs.

In the end, David recovered and even danced with me at my daughter's wedding a couple of months later, and didn't even need to use oxygen the whole day.

By March 2007, pneumonia settled into his lungs and again I thought he was going to die. His breathing had become very shallow and labored, and fluid was building up in his lungs. I was up early on a Saturday morning on the computer and "something" told me to go take a picture of David in the bedroom. I wasn't sure what was happening but I wasn't afraid.

The photo showed an angel and another being hovering above David. I took about five more incredible photos and then checked on David's oxygen. He was doing better, so I waited for him to get up. When he did wake up, he looked great. He walked without dragging his feet, and his oxygen numbers were great for the first time in two weeks. He had a few good weeks and then began getting worse again, unable to breathe while lying down. They drained fluid from his lungs but that didn't help. The lung doctor told me, "It's his heart, not his lungs." The heart doctor told me, "The lung doctor is wrong." And I was losing my mind.

To breathe, David was now standing almost all the time, and on five liters of oxygen 24/7, while taking breathing treatments every hour. Watching this kind of suffering, where David had to fight for every breath was the worst thing I ever had to do. I could do nothing to help him and felt beyond helpless. I know it's worse to watch a child suffer but watching anyone you love suffer like that is traumatic.

The lung doctor put David on a real strong water pill which helped David lose 20 pounds of fluid. I was working at a healing center that had a water ionizer that raises the pH in the body (making it more alkaline). I had David drink the ionized water as he was losing 20 pounds over the next week. Because of the extreme benefits of the water to the body, he is still only drinking this ionized water.

One day, a practitioner "just happened" to be visiting the healing center and he could diagnose a person's illness using a pendulum. He diagnosed that David had Congestive Heart Failure before either doctor ever did.

I also put him in a program called All-Inclusive Method, or AIM (see Appendix E). I tried everything, refusing to give up on helping David. When I knew his health was slipping away again, I called Cheryl to get a reading. She said, "It doesn't look good but John is asking you to turn David over to him."

As usual, I did, trusting that my son would intervene for our highest good. And he did. The heart doctor finally listened to me, gave David an echocardiogram and was able to see that he was in severe Congestive Heart Failure, so the proper heart medication was finally prescribed. With all these things, and the Good Lord above, David became better than ever in less than two months just like Jesus told Susan that he would. Both of the doctors remain in awe of his recovery.

Chapter Nineteen

My Camera Pierces the Veil

As all of this drama was unfolding, I discovered that my digital camera was able to photograph energy. I had always taken aura photos with special aura cameras but now I realized my ordinary digital camera would not only photograph orbs and strange things in the sky but also other phenomena. While in my healing room doing sessions with EFT and the tuning forks, I took pictures of my clients against a black backdrop, and amazing images of emotions and light beings would appear on the photos.

Once again, Susan entered the scene and asked me to photograph her jewelry. I would never have photographed anything except people if Susan hadn't asked. She channels her pieces of jewelry from Archangel Raphael, and had begun making jewelry after a near death experience as a child, almost drowning in Laguna Beach. To make her feel better, her mother had taken her to a bead store, and Susan started making jewelry. It became an obsession with her as a child, and jewelry making became a thriving business as an adult.

I spent the whole day photographing her pieces of jewelry, and when I'd finally finished and looked at the photos on the computer, I was shocked. I actually saw a side view of Jesus hanging on the cross in one of the photos. I had placed a necklace with a gorgeous cross on it over an angel and took a picture. The image of Christ on the cross above the necklace on the angel was crystal clear to me. (Part of the photo is on the back cover of the book). These images were not clear to everyone, but for sure to myself, Susan and David. Strangely, I wouldn't even have a crucifix in my home because to me, the crucifix portrayed the suffering Christ and I wanted only the Risen Christ in my view. After having my fill of that suffering aspect growing up as a Catholic, I didn't want to think about the suffering of Christ anymore. (I even gave away my replica of the Pieta because of the sadness and suffering of Jesus and Mary.) I had worked hard to eliminate the martyr program that had plagued me throughout my life. To me the cross was a symbol of the martyr and I was done with that.

I took the photo with the image of Christ on the cross with me one day as I was visiting a woman in a nursing home. She was a young woman who'd had a stroke and her husband didn't know what to do to help her. I told him, "This is my specialty," and went to see her. As I hung the photo in her room, I said, "The message in this picture is that all suffering has purpose." I knew those words were for me, too, and that the suffering in the world made me sad and added to my addiction to sadness. With the realization that there is always a higher purpose, I could detach from suffering, both personally and in the healing room. I could look at it through the eyes of my soul – the eternal part of me that could see the broader view of it. I could see suffering as the chief architect of our life, making us who we really are and fine-tuning our compassion. I am sure this detachment has helped me grow both as a practitioner in the healing arts and as the person who could emerge from John's death, alive and with purpose.

~ ~ ~

Through the months, the camera began to show faces and more intense energies every day. For example, it was common for a loved one from the other side to show up in a healing session. I started to photograph artwork, musical instruments, rocks, water, salt and anything I could think of. Images of faces became very common, not only faces of people who had passed over, but the faces of the artists who created the artwork. Other living people and pets would show up who were not in the room at the time the picture was taken.

I was asked to take photos of pictures of people who had passed away. Miraculous, impossible things were coming through, as if John was sending special healing colors for people through the camera. The camera was breaking the laws of physics daily. I could photograph right through people, with only a slight outline of their actual body. What would appear to be the image of the Blessed Mother would show up in the photos. People would see what they were meant to see. Each person would see completely different things than I would, as though there was a special message in the photos only they could see.

It became more revealing every day. Each time I thought I saw the most incredible photo the next one would be more astounding, as if the camera could hear me talk to it. I felt I was always talking to John when I worked with the camera. If I photographed the blank wall, it would give me a picture of my mood or feelings. I realized one day when my computer stopped working. I became frustrated and, in order to try and get a new photo into the computer, I took a picture of the blank wall. It was clear from the murky red and brown colors that my frustration was clearly coming through the camera. This helped me realize even more how our emotions affect the physical world around us. If our emotions can change the color of a wall, imagine what it can do to our health.

One night, I took a picture of David just watching TV. In the photo, the footrest was on the floor and also floating above his head and a golden light was shining down on David. The photo also showed a bright golden ball above his head and John's eyes looking down at him. I didn't bother to show the picture to David since I'm always making him get up and look at my new pictures on the computer. I decided to let him enjoy his show. When he came to bed, he told me of a visit he'd just had with John. In the past, he would ask me why John never came to him but just to me. Well, this latest photo was proof to me that John had just been waiting for some alone time with David to thank him for all he'd done for us.

I had become friends with moms who had lost their children and knew she could communicate with them. It was great to be around other "crazy" moms. For example, I met Xandra Graviet at a Transition Team class, taught by Steve Rother. She had written a book, *Angel in Disguise*, in which she channeled her daughter Brooke. I couldn't wait to get my hands on the book and devour it. I knew I could hear John, and I knew she also was hearing Brooke. The messages she received were so beautiful, and Xandra and I knew we would be working together some day but we could never quite figure out how.

One day, she sent me an email about our children wanting us to do something together with music, which didn't make sense to me because I'm not a musician and so many great people in the field are doing healing music. It just didn't click with me but I said, "Okay, let's get together and talk about it." As I was showing her some of the great healing music already available in the field and how I just couldn't see how we would fit into the picture, I heard John say, "Take her picture with the 'Holy Harmony' tuning forks." (I had these special forks in my healing room and hadn't used them yet. The forks I always used went directly on the meridian points. I thought these were better since they sent sound directly into the body. The Holy Harmony forks were to be used only around the head, which in my mind wouldn't be as effective so I never really used them.)

    I had Xandra listen to each fork on both sides of her head and I photographed her with each sound penetrating her energy field. The pictures had us both in shock. Although I had worked with her many times, I was never able to get to the core issue. I was able to see a transformation in her from the sound of the forks unlike anything I had ever seen or photographed. Her eyes changed along with her whole demeanor. It was as though all fear was released from her consciousness. It was clear and obvious that something very healing and dramatic had occurred within her. She verified that she felt the changes come over her.

    The camera was becoming my teacher and began showing me, through the photos I took during the sessions, so many truths about sound, healing and the dimensions of self. It taught me how connected we all are through our thoughts. In the many photos in which John came through, he would come through as the last photo of him I'd just looked at. If I had just seen a photo of him at age 14 in the hallway, that's the way he would show up in the next photo.

    One morning, I got up before dawn and began photographing the guitar John's friends had all signed and gave to us at his funeral. A picture of him in his casket came through on that photo. The energy of his death was heavy around that guitar.

    John's girlfriend, Dominique, came to Las Vegas for a visit almost two years after he died. She was still in a deep depression over his death. She stayed at my home because I knew if I kept her with me for a while and worked with her, John would be very present in the healing room. I knew with both of us there, his invisible embrace would become very visible, but I didn't know how.

During our first session, we were doing an algorithm for grief over the death of her grandmother who had shot herself, and the energy around that was especially heavy. One of the major points used in Energy Psychology is on the upper lip just below the nose. I am very careful at this point not to drop the forks because they are heavy and could bruise the face. The forks flew out of my hands and landed on her stomach. We both cracked up laughing because we knew it was John being funny. I immediately took two more pictures because I thought I could capture him laughing, and I was right. I always tell clients, "After a session, watch a funny movie to break up the heavy energy moving through the aura." John handled that for us.

The next time we went into the healing room, Dominique had a terrible toothache – a nine on a scale of one to ten. Since she doesn't live in Nevada, I decided to teach her how to heal herself so she would know how to do it. I wanted her to understand the power of our thoughts. I asked her, "Do you know the song, If you're happy and you know it, clap your hands?" She did. I told her to change the words to:

"I deeply and completely love myself, I deeply and completely love myself, even with this toothache, even with this tooth ache, and I deeply and completely love myself." I teach this whenever I work with children.

I went over all the major tapping points and told her to close her eyes and imagine tapping on the points while singing the song. Again she cracked up laughing after about one minute because she couldn't believe her toothache was gone. My camera picked up the shift in her energy field clearly in the photos. Even a novice without any experience in auras or energy could interpret these photos.

~ ~ ~

The first Christmas after John's death was a most challenging one. I always went to my daughter's house with John and David to watch the boys open presents, and I made no prediction to anyone, including myself, about how I would handle these family celebrations. I did not care what anyone thought about how I would navigate my way through those days.

I woke up Christmas morning and had every intention of going to the cemetery to visit John's grave. I hadn't been to the gravesite since the funeral, almost three months earlier. I gathered some things to leave at the site of his grave and got into the car. I heard John say, "Go to Jamie's, and be with the boys."

I felt him strongly push me away from the cemetery, so I drove to Jamie's and watched as the family opened their presents. In the photos of that morning, many strange images came through the camera. One particular picture looked as though my grandson and John had merged. Others showed intense energy in the auric field, and in one of Michelle, she was almost invisible.

I know this was the beginning of my focus on John's life with me as "John the spirit." Each time I drive past the road leading to the cemetery, I get a knot in my stomach. I hate that his body is rotting in the ground and that's the place people go to remember the dead. Being amidst all those rotting bodies is the place I least like to go to remember John. I remember him in music and photos and videos, but he is more alive to me now as every day goes on. I play with him in the healing room. I talk to him through my camera and fight with him at my computer the same way we did when he was alive. He has taught me many things on the computer both in person and in spirit, and even now I know he's pushing me further and further every day to prove there is no death.

John seems to be around and interacting with many people, not just me. I believe with all my heart God is everywhere and is within the cells of our body and our thoughts. He/She is the divine spark of creation that gives life to everything in the universe. If there is no death, and whatever we believe to be God dwells within us, then, how many other total contradictions are there?

If God is within us, then everything outside of us is unnecessary, and we have all the power to create our lives within us. How many beliefs and fears run our lives that we pay an enormous price for? When will we have the courage to ask, "Has what we believe been placed there by someone with an agenda that serves someone or something other than our highest good"?

Creativity and desire are the children of the divine spark within us that can never die. Only the body will perish. In winter, many things appear to die, only to blossom more beautifully again in spring. The "very conscious spirit" never dies and, according to John, seldom rests. Examining the fears and judgments we hold onto, and the price we pay to honor them, is the first step to re-igniting the divine pilot light within. Playing the game of forgetting who we are, only to remember again, who we really are, is the greatest reality series we can participate in. Becoming love and disarming fear is our only job.

Through the many sessions in the healing room, I became aware of the worst fears and judgments that run rampant in our minds. Within the framework of Energy Psychology, not only the emotions are dealt with but also the beliefs that do not benefit us. First they are accepted and then, by choice, replaced with a new and improved version of them. This can be done anywhere and anytime we take the opportunity to recognize a belief that limits us. That is the beauty of this modality.

It's free and anyone can learn and do it. It's not the only way, but it's certainly a quick and easy way.

Using the vibration of our voices or the imagination of our voices in our minds, we have the tools to heal the core of our deepest wounds. Our life lessons are structured around these beliefs and wounds so there is always an appropriate time for the beliefs and wounds to be revisited. The soul decides the "when, where and how" our issues will be dealt with, and rest assured, we cannot hide from them. I know this because I have tried to outsmart the system and it cannot be done. As a matter of fact, the harder we try to avoid the things that make us uncomfortable, the more likely we will be getting a visit from them. This may sound like a "Murphy's Law" attitude and it is, but it is also a universal law. The Buddha says: "What You Resist, Persists."

This is a great place to start to discover YOU. I find that one of the biggest issues for most people is being judged as foolish, naive or even worse, stupid. Being judged as unhealthy, fat, lazy or even old is a new fear, not to mention not having perfectly white teeth. A huge fear that surfaces is the fear of being and/or dying alone. Self-hatred or feeling unworthy is right up there in the top five.

Even the Dead Sea Scrolls addressed the inability to love oneself. It's interesting to know that these issues have been part of our evolution dating back thousands of years. I believe we are in a time when we can actually hear the truth and act upon it.

It's not within the scope of this book to teach Energy Psychology, but it's my intention to awaken you to the many applications and websites where you can learn everything about this incredible, free tool of self-discovery. I have included the web sites for the various modalities in the "References" section towards the back of the book. As you heal yourself, everyone you touch feels the shift and the ripple effect never stops. As my daughter Michelle said, "The one thing I learned from John's death is that we are all connected."

Chapter Twenty

Pre-Birth Planning

I know that souls spend the heavenly equivalent of many earth-years planning every aspect of their upcoming incarnation, and those plans involve meeting with the souls who will incarnate to become your parents and siblings. I was eager to learn about the plans that I, John Sr. and John made, and what we hoped to get out of our incarnations. For example, did we intend that John Sr. would take on such an abrasive personality, and why? On August 8, 2007, I had the long-awaited reading with Cheryl to learn more about John's pre-birth planning. I was excited and had a good idea what to expect, having taken classes from Steve Rother in Transitions and Spiritual Psychology. Also, I had just finished reading Courageous Souls about thirteen people with very challenging lives. The author had different mediums look at each of their pre-birth planning secessions. Each medium explained why they had built so many challenges in their lives.

As always Cheryl began with a prayer, and then her guides began speaking:

Mother Father God, we thank you for this gathering and are open only to the light.

Greetings Beloved. Today will be a day of what you call the education of that which is beyond the physical. By education we are referring to the fact that spirit comes into the physical to express itself. We come in to express through certain scenarios that we set up for ourselves. We have forgotten, while in the physical, certain aspects of what is truly us as spirit, and also what we have planned. This is what you call the pre-incarnational planning.

Pre-incarnational planning is simply that. It is simply looking at what has been misspoken or misunderstood in previous physical incarnations, and using physical life as an opportunity to correct those misunderstandings and give ourselves the opportunity to come once more fully into spirit. And so each of us plans a life with many, many choices.

You could look at life planning as a huge tapestry, one that would cover the wall of this room and much, much more, and each thread is an option within that plan. There are literally billions of threads within each tapestry of life, and each is an option. And although we may plan a specific tapestry when coming in, it is almost guaranteed that, in the physical, the tapestry will be shifted due to our free will. It is one of the reasons we leave ourselves so many options and so many connections.

As has already been given through so many sources, when we are doing our planning for any incarnation, there are many souls involved. The souls involved are not just those of the higher consciousness, but also those who learn and grow with us. You call them your "soul group." In that soul group are individuals with similar goals and many experiences together, not just in the physical plane but also through all dimensions and throughout time. We gather together with us these individuals whom we love so well and so dearly, to assist us in our journey of remembering who we are while we are in the physical.

We will draw an analogy. Think of the Masters – Jesus, Buddha, Krishna, Quan Yin and many others. These are individuals who have come in and fully remember spirit while in the physical body. It's as simple as that. That is what we are doing. Our goal is to become, as you say, the Gods that we are. And we do this in thought, word and deed through our choices and our actions.

Now, there are many times when we hear the question, "Why _____?" Why does this happen? This is a very important question if it is aimed at the soul purpose, if it causes one to rise higher in questioning and higher in understanding. This is what we are to address today.

There are many whys. A part of us has made many such agreements in a number of lifetimes with the one known in this lifetime as Regina. A trust has built through these sequences. This is what you call a "refining lifetime"; some call it a Master level lifetime. The one through whom we speak (Cheryl) calls it "the Ph.D. course."

It is a coming together, a refining of, what you think of there as the harder lessons in life. Those lessons that require absolute unconditional love and acceptance of Divine Will as your own will, in order to move through them and remain in love.

The agreement was made between these two to come in as son and mother. Because of the specific dynamics between the mother and the child, let us first look at the one you know as John. John had dealt with a number of lifetimes where he was, as you say, dragged down by outer circumstances. These outer circumstances were, you would think of it as, the higher soul vibrations meeting the lower soul vibrations, almost as if there is a short circuit when this happens.

There were three lifetimes wherein John crossed over with the feeling of defeat, with the feeling of sorrow. Not sorrow for himself, but for what he saw going on in the form of the human. He knew it was not who we really are, and he could not understand the choices others were making. He could not understand the choices he made either because of being brought down into that vibration. So what was most important to him in this lifetime was addressing the sorrow. To be able to see what is right about what is happening in the human form, rather than to compare it to spirit and say, something is wrong here.

He asked in this lifetime to be able to see the divinity that is in the sentient life forms making up the earth plane. And so he came in with the love of music. Music, as you know, is one of the languages of what you call the angelic realms. It is one of the key languages of the higher realms. The love of music allowed us, on the other side, to share as much as possible the joy of spirit with John while he was here with the veil dropped. It was chosen very specifically.

You and he met to discuss the music because it was a rather risky way of keeping the connection, because of what happens with the music here in this earth plane at the time he was to incarnate. And as the two of you met, he expressed his relief and his pleasure of having this knowing of music. This pursuit of music kept keep him connected and bring the joy back into life. But at the same time it was brought out by the teachers and by you, Regina, that in the earth plane, what we think of as the musical industry was coming into a time period that was not positive. It was, in fact, rather destructive in probably eighty percent of the people involved. And so there was a caution in here. And you told John that you would be the one to help him stay connected with spirit, and grounded in spirit.

Some say "grounded in spirit" is an oxymoron. It is spiritual grounding. It is however, as you know, an absolute essential. We must be grounded in love for the earth plane and all life forms here, for it is all sentient, while at the same time being grounded in our spiritual knowing. That is how we express spirit.

You told him, "I will have some doubts about the direction your music takes, but I will never have doubt about you. I will have doubts about the direction the music takes, to try to help guide you to a kinder softer level of your joyous expression, so that it does not become a part of the anger and the rage being expressed through music in the earth plane at the time you and I are there."

It was seen that this inclination toward expression of the negative – the "not love" rather than the love – was to grow stronger in the earth plane as John grew up. And so you, Regina, made the promise that you would assist him as much as he would allow you, to move his music in the direction of joy in spirit by being that spiritual influence. And yet you are also the mom, which is why you brought in the combination of the practical, down-to-earth, along with the extreme joy in spirit.

We would digress just a moment if you would, between the relationship you chose between you and the one you chose as your husband, who is the father of John. This relationship was specifically to assist you in the qualities you needed to help John make different choices and perceive differently in his lifetime. What you did with the one who fathered John is what we call trial-by-fire. There is the old saying: "The greatest and strongest and brightest swords come through the hottest fire." You agreed to this for many reasons and, of course, there are many other reasons, but we will deal with the specifics relating to you and John.

The specifics are that the trauma you would go through in the marriage with this individual, John Sr., whom you love dearly on the other side would strengthen you in your faith because that is the only place you would have to turn. Of course, when we have free will, you can decide to become bitter and angry, but you have been through that already, and it was seen that you are in a perfect position to choose spirit instead. And so you said, "I will go through this." There are many other reasons, but this is one of them. And in having to turn more towards spirit and more towards self, you learned through opposites.

In that marriage, you did not have a support system. You did not have an acknowledgement of who you are and what your truth is. And so you had to cling tightly to your truth yourself. You had to be your truth. And this gave you the strength you needed to share this with John, and to be able to go through the trauma of seeing your child at risk.

Now, you recognized John when he was born, just as he recognized you. You have been so many things to each other. Let us tune into more of the specific planning between you, John and some of the others directly involved.

It is seen among you, John and John's father, that the continued influence by John's father on a day-to-day basis would not be the most advantageous for the three of you. And so it is agreed that if John's father does not change his personality while he is there, there will be a parting of the ways at a very young age.

John is talking to his father. "I have seen cruelty and unkindness in the world and it has caused me great sorrow and I have not been able to stand up to it" (in the sense of not being able to bring the sorrow out of his heart). He has, of course, stood up to it in the sense of fighting it, not accepting it but never in the sense of seeing the divine purpose behind it while he was in the physical. And so he looks at his father and says, "The personality you are choosing reflects well my version of what the earth plane is like while I am in the physical. You will help me greatly by giving me the opportunity to look at it every day and to see where I fit. To see what is true and what is not. To give me the chance to stop trying to be acceptable to the physical definition of life."

And the father agrees. "I am going in with a personality that will take on the characteristics where I do control through the physical. I believe in the material." He chuckles here and says, "It is my God in this lifetime." And he adds, "I will do this for you. I would ask in return that you do not allow it to go so far that it takes you where you were in the previous lifetimes." And John considers this.

The teachers come forward and say, "The greatest way to handle this is among the three of you. This is where the agreement about the separation comes in." And the agreement is made. The father says to John, "What you will allow me is that, through you, I can know the essence of spirit. I can know the presence of joy in the form of music. Simply the fact that you are coming in as an artistic soul."

John promises his father, "I will continue to try to show you what real love is – unconditional love and acceptance. I will do my very best to hang on to that and to try to share it with you."

His father says, "I will try to open to this but I can't guarantee it. I am taking on a personality that is very tough but I will try to open to it and I will continue to give you opportunities to learn the love that you are, and that YOU ARE THE LOVE regardless of what is around you." This is a key point John wants, so this agreement is made.

You are entering into this discussion also. You are looking at John's father and say, "I love you very much, but let's make this clear. In this lifetime, I am a mother, I am a healer, and I would love to be the healer for you also, but with the personality you are taking on, it may be that you are the one who teaches me to walk away."

John's father accepts this. "Yes, I will be happy to do this for you. It is not something I wish to do because I know it will feel unloving in the physical. But I also know that as the healer, there must be a level of discernment learned, where you know when to walk away."

This one (Cheryl) calls it Divine Detachment. It is unconditionally loving that person from somewhere else. Whether they are close to you or far away does not matter. It is loving them for the soul they are, without allowing the personality to have a detrimental effect on the actions and thoughts.

So this agreement is made between the two of you. You both look at John and ask, "Do you understand this?" Of course John does. He has been following and he has been nodding and all three are in agreement on this.

Now, there is also a sister coming in. She (Michelle) comes in and says, "I too have been dealing with the sorrow of the earth plane, only my sorrow has come through as anger, and sometimes by being beaten down in trying to be what someone else says I am supposed to be, and by denying myself and what I know is right to simply try to win approval. I would come in as the daughter and the sister if this is acceptable to you."

And everyone says, "Let's discuss this." We can see on their faces there is an agreement that this might be a very good thing. She says, "In several lifetimes, I have done what I was told to do when I knew it was wrong for me, and I crossed over in those lifetimes still not knowing who I was, or what was real and what wasn't. In this lifetime, I would like to come in as a woman, because that is the form I took in these other lifetimes of which I speak. And because it is a foil, it is the feminine energy for this soul (John) whom I love dearly."

The session then included much discussion between John Sr. and Michelle, which is not included here.

Looking between John and his sister, we see much love for many, many centuries. His sister looks at him and says, "I will try to help you stay for as long as you need to stay. I will be your other support. Your mother is on one side, I'll be on the other, and you'll lean on us, and I'll lean on you." John looks at her and says, "The degree of sorrow I bring in with me is extreme, and I'm going to allow myself to feel this but I don't want this to have a negative impact on you." Michelle smiles very brightly and says, "You know very well it won't. It's exactly what I need."

And you step in, Regina, and say, "I'll be the buffer for this. I'll be the one who watches the balance." They both look at you and say, "Yes." We will, of course, all three watch the balance, we will all three participate, but if you will agree to be the one, sort of like an angelic referee, not in the sense of breaking up a fight, but in the sense of watching the reactions back and forth, and bringing balance back into the situation."

They are smiling very broadly because you have the look on your face of a very determined soul, with her hands on her hips and tapping her foot, saying, "I will take care of this." This is an aspect of the personality you will bring in with you. You are already demonstrating it. It's not in the sense of impatience but in the sense of knowing rightness and determination. It is an absolute knowing, "I will make it so."

Cheryl asked me, "Are there specific questions you would like to ask about these dynamics?"

I replied, "Did it work out the way we had hoped"?

Yes, it is seen as a triumph on this side. There were a number of options that would have been acceptable, ranging anywhere from "Okay" to "Hallelujah." And what we got here was "Hallelujah" because one of the possibilities that were seen was suicide because of the sorrow. John was determined he would bring in the sorrow strongly enough to force himself to see the beauty, because he would have no choice. When a soul decides to do this, there is the danger of the soul leaving by its own will, rather than by divine will. That was the worst-case scenario.

Now the absolute "Halleluiah" Hail Mary would be that the father would turn around, realize the loving spirit he is while in the physical, and that John would bring music into his life in the manner of joy, and go with a different crowd. And that you would continue in your work with these three by your side. We achieved close to that in this lifetime.

Let us look at the manner of John's crossing. This was a chosen exit because of the progress that had been made. You had noticed the sorrow that had been a part of John for so long was lifting. There were signs, like when there are a lot of clouds and the sun peeks through. There were extended periods of the sun peeking through for John, and he was beginning to understand the earth plane not as hostile, alien and wrong, but rather more of a neutral feeling. We wish to move into Divine Love but that neutrality always seems to come first for us when we are in the physical. It was a huge step. The manner of crossing was not suicide; it was what you call accidental, however it was a chosen exit. The manner was alone so no one could stop it, because otherwise someone would have. There is so much determination in the love for John here.

Cheryl pauses as she taps into that love.

Let us speak of what is gained in each individual in this lifetime through the presence and the crossing of John. In the presence of John, his father was given the opportunity to lighten up, to come outside of the personality he had chosen, to recognize and grasp the Divine Love offered through a child. That child would like to give unconditional love, unconditional acceptance, and that is what John kept offering to his father over and over again, and this was a great opportunity. It did not make a large change from the physical view but it did make a change from the spiritual view.

Now what is gained between brother and sister as a result of John's crossing over is she has actually started to create exactly what you, Regina, have been creating. More fully embracing the inner self, becoming curious of what is beyond what she sees, hears, feels and tastes, and it is because John has crossed over.

Another issue brought up for the sister is that there were some feelings of guilt. On this side in the planning, she had agreed to try to help keep him here. There is a soul memory of this, so there is a feeling within her of: "I should have seen it coming. I should have known. I should have done ____." That is the memory of the pre-birth planning. She played her role as she was meant to. It is now her responsibility, according to her soul, to use this crossing to get curious and to start looking at her own control of her own life. For she saw John, and in many cases felt he was out of control. That he could not find the point of control in his life. That he couldn't find the balance. That's really what we are looking for when we say control. We're looking for harmony and balance. And she felt he did not have his.

She was a loving, supporting sister, and took on some of the sorrow. She brought some in herself in the form of saying,

"I must be wrong. I should do what society tells me to do, I should fit in." And then in her love for John, she took on a little more of that sorrow. And this is well, this is a good thing, for it brings it to the point where she will begin to look at it, she already has. And she continues to grow through this experience exponentially. We can see the growth on the soul level where she begins to question what is presented to her as truth when it does not resonate with her deeper sense of truth. This is a very good thing.

Now what is gained by the mother? The mother has come in to live a life of service. And she stated very clearly in the pre- birth planning that YES, she would be of service to her family, but above all to be of service to Divine Love. Her main purpose was to clear the way for that Divine Love to manifest through the earth plane in whatever way came up. And that is one of the reasons you see the interest in so many different means of healing. In working with John, Regina was faced with the necessity of exploring every option possible for helping this soul whom she loved so dearly. And in doing so, she expanded her own consciousness because she knew she could not find what she needed in the physical. This was a keynote for the relationship between these two. Her love for John forced her to look beyond what is already known. Even beyond what was known in the spiritual, for she could not find it there. It also strengthened the turning within that had begun several lifetimes before. It strengthened it, for there was nowhere else to turn.

Look at the scenario. She is the mother, with three children and a husband. The husband does not turn within; the husband does not glow with unconditional love. The husband is a challenge. She cannot go to the children for help for she feels, "I am the mother. I am the one who helps them." So she has put herself in a position where she must go within. And she does. And what has happened in the crossing over of John is actually a strengthening of her faith and an agreement.

A part of the pre-incarnational agreement was that one of the options was John leaving early before Regina. In that option, it was agreed the two would work very closely as a team on the work to be done here in the physical. Because they had the connection in the physical of going through the same physical body and being so close, nurturing and supporting each other, it makes for a very dynamic connection from spirit to physical. It is a little known fact that when a child comes through a woman's body that connection is never lost regardless of circumstances. Many don't understand that it is actually a spiritual, psychic, kinetic connection that science will one day be able to see and prove. When you have this kind of a strong connection in the physical and one crosses over to the spiritual, that kinetic dynamic energy remains. It is altered only in the sense of "GROWING MORE POWERFUL."

Now the key. If the one who stays behind is open to the new relationship, it becomes dynamic and powerful beyond physical ability to measure. However if the one who stays in the physical goes fully into grief and yearns for the old relationship, with no recognition of the new relationship, the energy is then passive. It is still present but not active because it is not acknowledged and not used.

One of the important things we would like to help bring through in this relationship for many, many people is to shift the awareness of crossing over. It is a new relationship. An unlimited relationship, if we can accept it as such. And as we begin to learn to do this, the entire social structure will shift. It will be spiritually enlightening because the fear will be taken care of. It will be no more.

In this pre-incarnational agreement, it was decided that John would wait to leave until after his teens because it was felt there was too much work to be done that may not be done successfully in his younger years. That's why there were a couple of close calls. It was determined that what the two of you here were doing together had not yet been sufficiently accomplished for him to leave. It was going in a positive direction, but still with much to learn and do. And John felt he had much to contribute. He was quite pleased with what he was learning as he progressed through twelve to sixteen. He shows this in pulling himself out of quicksand, breaking the gravitational pull. This was an extremely important time for him.

Let us allow John to speak for us.

"It was so much more important for me to experience coming out of the hopelessness over that extended period, by making some wrong choices, for I did make what we would think of as wrong choices in the physical. It was through these not so happy choices that I came face to face with the fact that I could either begin to see the good things in life, or I could perish. I don't mean to be dramatic, but this is how we look at it when we're in the depths, as you say. And so you could see I was beginning to make better choices as we come into fifteen and sixteen and so on.

"You can also see the influence of the friends I chose. Some of these friends were in the same place I was trying to escape from the sorrow, the pain and the confusion. Just trying to get away, that's all. Not trying to understand it or gain control of it, because at that point, we didn't see the possibility of gaining control. We didn't know it was us. But then I began to allow some individuals in with a lighter, more hopeful frame of mind. These individuals assisted with watering seeds already planted in my family life. And you can see, those of you who are close to me, that as I progressed in the last couple of years in my life, even though there were a couple of periods that were a little scary in the physical, I was on my way up. I was beginning to accept there might be something better behind what I saw in the physical. I was beginning to lighten up on myself, on life. There is even a shift in my music, in the lyrics, that is noticeable.

"Part of the reason this is done is to leave behind some of the physical signs of the changes going on within. I was not one to openly share my grief with many. Or my pain. There were a chosen few who knew what I was hiding. And this is well. For as a part of my planning before coming in, I asked that I not add to the sorrow already in the earth plane. That I not be one of the downers. To do that, it was necessary to take on a personality that would not allow myself to spew the hopelessness. I thought, I must take care of this myself, or with those chosen few. And I am well pleased with the outcome. For even with the friends I chose, who had the confusion and the sorrow I did, I didn't share the anger, the resentment, the sorrow. I shared laughter whenever I could. I KNEW SOMEHOW IT WAS UP TO ME TO LOOK FOR THE WAY. And yes, we shared stories of hard times and disappointments, but I'm very pleased with that part of the lifetime. And for those who do not understand the pleasure of spirit as compared to the pleasure in the physical, pleasure of spirit verses pleasure of ego, pleasure of ego says, 'Look what I have done. Aren't I marvelous?' Pleasure of spirit says, 'Look what I have been allowed to assist in creating. Look what I have been a part of. It is humbleness, a joy, and exhilaration.' This is the pleasure I know."

Now let us once again now merge and speak as one voice. Is the answer sufficient for the question?

"Would it be possible to address the specifics of the night he died? His agreement with Alex and Jack?" I asked.

Yes. Alex and Jack are not just good friends on this side; they are good friends on the other side. Alex and Jack agreed if it came to the point were he was going to take this exit, they would assist him. It is already known that the death was accidental. However, it could not have happened if the circumstances had not been set up exactly the way they were. Everyone is very clear on this. His friends were a part of the path that was more in keeping with the sorrow brought through in the music. It's a push-pull. They attempted to come together to assist each other to bring joy and happiness in the music, but the three of them were carrying the sorrow.

It was agreed they would accidentally set things up for John to use. It was agreed that John would be alone. But please note that he had his friends with him first. This was also part of the agreement. These two individuals would not agree to assist John in this way unless they could also be there to help him, be there to support him, be there for him. The primary purpose of this friendship was specifically to work through finding the joy inherent within the music. In making this final exit, these two gave the service of appearing to be at fault. Through negligence or thoughtlessness, it doesn't matter. But they said to John, "We allow ourselves to experience this because we love you and because it is some thing we need."

Each of these individuals was on a path of, you would say, not being extremely responsible. And each had asked for wake-up calls all along their life path to help them wake up to the fact that they didn't want to just drift through life like they had before. They had done it many times.

Let us go into the pre-birth again and look at John, Jack and Alex. The three are all talking about the fact that they have had several lifetimes where they just drifted through, with no strong sense of purpose, just simple distraction and trying to get away from the sorrow, the pain and the anger. The three of them look at each other and say, "The three of us would like in this lifetime to WAKE UP. To begin to live consciously, willfully, spiritually and become aware of life while we are in the physical."

The three look at each other and John says, "I have made the agreement with my mother that I will cross over before her. The three of us could become close friends. We could assist one another in this."

There is a pause here because John is very seriously considering what he is about to offer. He looks at the other two and says, "If you're willing, and we become close friends, if you have not taken the wake up calls you've received before, then you could directly participate in my crossing over."

Both individuals look at this and respond very quickly. They are very serious about this, and are nodding their heads, saying yes. This would serve the three of us. It is a wake-up call. Now both Jack and Alex hope they will use a different means of waking up because they know that this extreme wake-up has some dangers in it. When we are in the physical and we take this kind of a wake-up call, it is very possible that we will not use it to look within but rather to run away. To take the sorrow and the pain we had known before and actually fall into it and make it worse.

That is one of the reasons John thought about it before offering it. The purpose of their participation is for them to wake up, as John's sister wakes up. It is for them to start taking responsibility for their lives, not in a sense of having a haircut and getting a job, but in the sense of being responsible for what they create. Of consciously and willfully knowing how they create. Of knowing their purpose, which is a very great gift to give.

And so these three dear friends have come together in this drama. John, who speaks as one with us, is trying to assist them. We have the one who has gone back into the fear, back into the trying to escape because of the pain. We have the other who is beginning to come out. And yet it is still seen that both of these individuals are using John's crossing over to bring themselves to the point where they have no choice but to look into themselves. One is doing it by increasing the sorrow, pain and confusion; the other is beginning to come out of that. And it is seen that both are setting things up to gain from this, for they are dear friends and we on this side continue to assist. Can we bring through greater understanding on this?

"Yes," I replied.

John expresses his extreme love and gratitude to these two dear friends who put themselves in this situation for him. They offered to live an event that those of us in the physical would do anything to escape. They are sorting through guilt, sorrow, anger, judgment and the pain of loss as a result of what they have helped to create. As we have said, this is what this one calls a "Ph.D. life." They are both now at the point where they can do the turnaround very quickly, if they so choose. These are old and very determined souls.

"Yes. He could have left through two other means just prior to this exit, one a car accident and one somehow getting arrested for something he didn't do. What would make the determination on the other side of the veil not to choose those?"

A big part of that choice was not so much John, as how others could be helped in this decision. It was seen that Jack and Alex could gain greatly from being participants in John's crossing. When they were looking at the possibility of the car accident, everything was too indirect. John felt he could not assist others except indirectly. And so he said, "It might be easier that way but not better that way."

All souls came together and very seriously looked at this during the accident and agreed that it would be more advantageous in another way. So the exit is there and then it's gone.

Due to problems in the tape, I will give my best remembrance of the rest of the information.

As for the possibility on September 14, when John could have been arrested and ultimately died in jail, that option was also discarded because it would not have served the highest good for all at that time. It was my last choice, even on the other side of the veil, due to the emotional trauma John would have had to live through. I agreed to do it only if it was for the highest good for all. When that option was discarded, Alex and Jack were brought in to see if all were still in agreement to fulfill this exit. All were in agreement that this was for the highest good. John could have opted out of this exit, but there was so much to be gained from it.

My final question to spirit was about choices to stay in the physical after the quality of life was greatly diminished, such as living in a nursing home in various states of consciousness. That answer from spirit was: "That is usually a gift to allow others to serve."

Many different scenarios were explained how this was a gift to children and to society. My perception was shifted to such a great degree after that beautiful explanation. It always amazes me how differently things are seen on the other side.

When we are open to view things from a higher perspective, we can accept so much more easily what we resist so strongly on this side. Each and every soul chooses their exit for the highest good for all. There is so much beauty in this, and so much planning for the exit that it feels to me we should start to perceive death as the most beautiful and creative part of our life. It is comforting when we come into the truth that we are all connected as the woven threads in the tapestry and every soul realizes this as part of the re-entry into the heavenly planes and experiences the sweetness in leaving the body.

Chapter Twenty-One

My Gift from John: The Pink Ball of Light

On October 25, 2007, I went to bed as usual except I took my favorite picture of John and lit a candle next to it to look at while I went to sleep. Again at three o'clock in the morning, (obviously their favorite time to play on the other side), John woke me up and told me to photograph the moon. By now I use two digital cameras that capture things unseen by the naked eye. Intuitively I knew to use my new 10 megapixel digital camera. I love the moon over the lake with the mountains in the background so I was eager to fulfill his request. The moon was huge, almost full, and getting ready to set over the mountain range. As I began to take the pictures, I could see some energy in the camera and a very noticeable pink ball of light. I checked to see if I could see this ball of light when not looking through the camera viewfinder. It was not there. I took a number of photos and realized that I could, with my intention, move the pink ball of light. First, it was next to the moon. After taking several shots, I realized it was moving with the camera. As long as the moon was in the viewfinder screen, the pink ball was there. I could move it from right next to the moon to inside the lake area. I then aligned it perfectly between the moon and the moon's reflection on the lake. It was a beautiful picture.[1] I was beside myself at having discovered this new interactive aspect of the camera. I didn't know what I should do about this at three in the morning so I just took another bath and went back to bed. I knew that the next day I would look at the photos more closely on the computer.

The next day, as I was looking at these photographs of the pink ball of light on the computer and explaining to David what happened, Susan called with her usual opening line, "I had a dream about you and John last night." By now I just said, "Go" and she starts, always as excited as I am about whatever adventure John takes us on. She told me he came to her last night in a huge pink ball of light above a burning candle. It had not occurred to me until then that the pink ball of light could be John. I was thinking maybe it was an angel or some type of energy. She said his face was clear and he was speaking softly so she could barely hear him. She was so excited to be able to see him that she didn't really care what he was saying. We were both so excited about this that we were not coherent.

That evening, when the moon came out, I was thrilled to discover that the pink ball of light was still visible in the camera and could be seen by others. I could still photograph it and it was now also appearing in my other camera. As I was photographing, I asked David to come outside so I could get him in the picture. After taking a few more pictures, I decided to blend the pink ball of light with David. I directed the camera so that the pink ball of light would blend with his image. As I took the picture, I thought I'd broken the camera because David's image in the picture came out blurry; almost like a "see through" image. Also, I felt a terrible sadness that I couldn't figure out. The sadness was intense and washed over me or ran through me.

---

1   The moon and the pink ball of light appear on the cover just to the right of my face.

Later that evening when I took my bath, I put my favorite picture of John where I could see him above the bathtub and lit a candle. I took a picture of them and to my complete surprise the pink ball of light was again in the camera viewer and I could move it around in the camera viewfinder. I looked into the flame and could see John's face, so I asked him what had happened when I blended the pink light with the image of David. I heard him say (in my head, not my human ears), "I was so sad because David didn't know I touched him." Wow, I thought. They must miss human touch on the other side of the veil.

Again, I was awakened at three a.m. but I wasn't the slightest bit surprised. I got out of bed and went to see if the pink light was still in the camera viewer, and it was. The moon was again beautiful and I tried to direct the pink ball of light from the moon into my hand. I was so ecstatic that I could do that and film it as a movie as well as take pictures. When the pink ball of light moved into my hand, I had a warm feeling. I think John wanted me to know what it feels like when he touches me.

I noticed that anytime I have a dark place and light a candle, I could call him in as a pink light. I began using John in my healing sessions and the photos of my clients have very specific colors in them, almost like a tiny stained glass window. I decided to re-photograph photos of people I knew were sick using the pink ball of light. The first time I did this, I didn't tell the person what I had done but they left me a message saying they knew John had started to work with them at the exact moment I took the photo. Several reports of deep healings have taken place that I attribute to photographing photos of people with the pink ball of light, even if they are not present or don't know I've done this. I have only been working with this light for one month at the time of writing, however I will be keeping track for my own research.

I was pondering the meaning of the pink light and came up with the idea that it might be connected to rose crystal. I asked Susan what she thought about sending the sound from the tuning forks through crystals onto the meridian points used for EFT. We talked about the many ways this could be done and decided to try a session adding the crystals to the forks. Susan came to my house and brought her son Ryan and with a beautiful rose quartz crystal the size of a quarter. It was small enough to use with a tuning fork.

She did a session on her son while I photographed it. Her son, Ryan, had had back problems for a long time and his back hurt "really bad." On a scale of 1 – 10, he said it was an 8. I directed Susan to use the two forks, one at a time on the spine near the pain. She did this three times, which took about three minutes. Ryan said he could really feel the vibration using the rose quartz crystal. This was not the first time I worked with Ryan using tuning forks so he was quite aware of the difference of the intensity. He just said, "My back is fine." We then did the same thing on an issue he was angry about at school. Susan held the crystal and the forks on Ryan, and Ryan thought about his issue. She placed the crystal and tuning forks on six specific locations on his body and, within three minutes, he couldn't even get upset about the issue.

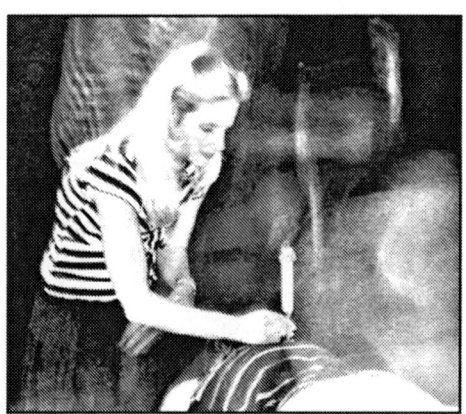

I was sure that the pink light was guiding us to conclude that by sending sound through frozen light, i.e., crystals, I can again accelerate the healing process. This system is so simple that all moms can learn it, and it works on physical pain and emotional problems. Energy Psychology is doing a documentary called: *Try It on Everything*. Everything you can heal through Energy Psychology can be amplified by the use of sound and light. We are energy and vibrations.

On Sunday, November 3, 2007, David and I were working on a project and he asked me to come downstairs and look at the sky. It was about three in the afternoon and the sky was very cloudy but the sun was peering through the clouds and it was vibrating with so much energy, it looked as if it was dancing. This sight was so unusual that I got both cameras and started taking pictures and movies of the sky. I had seen the sun dance on three other occasions but this was by far the most spectacular. We were both so exhausted after viewing the phenomena that I didn't even have the strength to look at the pictures on the computer. We were in kind of a daze for the rest of the day.

The next morning when I viewed the pictures on the computer, I was *not* surprised that there were many faces in the clouds in the sky, not just John's. The cloud formation was one I had never seen before. I am not quite sure of the significance of all of this but I have a channeling scheduled with Cheryl for the next Sunday morning. The session is set for 10:30 a.m., and as I put that on my calendar, I noticed the date would be November 11. That means we will be speaking at 11:11 a.m. on 11/11. So that's two double elevens, certainly not a coincidence. We had nothing to do with that timing, but I feel very strongly John and the higher realms did.

~ ~ ~

On Saturday November 24, I attended the monthly broadcast of the Virtual Light Broadcast with Steve Rother. He asked if anyone in the audience had a question to ask the Group. I waited but no hands went up. I had never had the courage to ask a question before but I was curious about the pink ball of light and the seemingly incredible healings. I asked Steve if the Group could address what the pink ball of light was doing.

Through Steve, the Group said, "Healing. Healing is happening. It's simple. So simple it's complicated for you because you try to understand everything but the reality is, the truth is always incredibly simple and uncomplicated. Is your son, John, actually performing these healings? The answer is yes. Yes, he is. You bet! He's creating a space for people to heal themselves. That is our definition of what a healer is – a person who creates space for other people to feel comfortable enough to heal or change themselves in some fashion. That's the biggest part of what the healer is. You provide the space for him to come through, which is what you have been doing personally. That is what your life has been focused on the last couple of years, ever since he left. And literally you have created the space for him to come in and do his work even though he did not get to do it in that fashion while he was here. That is a huge energy circle from his perspective. Now from the other perspective, what's happening from the people who are getting the healings? Can we expect miracles out of this? Absolutely, absolutely. It is a pinhole through the veil and you've got a whole lot of light on the other side. When you make any type of a pinhole in the veil like that, you're going to see interactions. If you can look at that pink ball of light, you can create a miracle in the space that John has created through you."

Chapter Twenty-Two

Revelations of the Tapestry

Sunday morning 11/11 arrived and I was well prepared for my conversation with John through Cheryl. He and I had decided long before what the main topic of the channeling would be. He knew I wanted some help for:

1. Teens and young adults who already are, or are thinking of, abusing prescription drugs, and
2. Parents who do not know what to do when they realize their children have already started.

The epidemic is so far reaching that the subject must be addressed. John's friends admitted looking in their parent's medicine cabinets as early as ten years old for any medication that read, "Will cause drowsiness" on the label, and just taking them for fun. John had done this but I had no idea he had. We never had prescriptions in the house until David needed them after his heart operation. I felt safe, but I wasn't. We lived in a good area with all nice kids and parents, and someone in the neighborhood is likely to have a prescription for Xanax or an old bottle of painkillers lying around. In Las Vegas, Oxycontin is freely prescribed for pain, as are many other highly addictive substances, making this city more vulnerable than most. I wanted to hear what John had to say from the vantage point of the higher realms because so many of our brightest and best are losing the battle through addiction or worse.

I set the healing room up with cameras, video and sound, as well as my three digital cameras. We got started at about 10:45 with special prayers. Then Cheryl began:

Let us first greet our beloved friends, our loved ones on this side that you call the physical. Let us set the tone for this gathering as one of joyous celebration for, in this earth plane, death is looked upon as tragedy, as a loss. Yet the message that is being brought forth in this work is that death is simply a transition and there is always a purpose in it. Always there is greater purpose, and there is much grander LOVE.

We would ask that this gathering be held in the spirit of the celebration of Divine Love. This is a celebration of the coming together of all children of God. The one you call John blesses our group with his presence. He has asked that several of us speak with him. He will be coming through as you know. There will be others such as the Master and Angelic realms, of course, present as invited.

We would speak summarily on what you would call The Elusive Gift of Tragedy. Death is perceived as an ending, a very scary thing, for we know not what occurs after the physical body stops, after the heart is no longer beating and the physical eyes no longer see. So those of us who are left behind do not recognize the new form that has been taken. It is very important that people understand that a part of the message of this book is: "A NEW FORM IS TAKEN." Actually it is the old form, it is the truth of who we are, in much lighter bodies and much lighter spirits, with laughter, love and communion. And so in this book, we attempt to bring forth the message of the JOY of death, and the fact that the method of crossing always has a purpose. The method of crossing is chosen not just for the individual who returns home, but rather for everyone who is in the sphere of that individual. It is to have an influence of some sort on everyone who has close contact with the one who is coming HOME. You will notice that when we speak of what you call death, we will simply call it coming HOME.

You think of it as desirable or not desirable, but on this side, we see the purpose of everything. Even when a choice is made, one says, "Oh dear, that one will pay for that choice." Yes, that one will pay in the sense of not knowing who he or she is, but not in the sense of retribution, simply in the sense of choosing differently the next time. And, as usual, we have set up the plane of opposites, the duality. When we make what we think of as the wrong choice, we discover through experience the wrongness of that choice. We discover it does not fit, it does not feel good, and it does not have good repercussions. And in that knowing, we become twice as strong in the knowing of what is good. That is the purpose behind many of what you call wrong choices.

Now we would return once again to the crossing of John, our dear friend. We would speak of the mental and emotional processes of the individual you knew as John. In coming into this particular physical body, one of the many themes being addressed was the feeling of helplessness, with no way out. It is one of the reasons this one was born into this particular family. When there were troubled times, and the teenage activities sometimes involving alcohol, drugs, driving too fast, or speaking unkindly, there was a feeling within of desperation. We release now to the one you knew as John.

John: I will speak first directly of the mental and emotional processes within the physical body. In the family to which I was born, I saw the opposites and the extremes. I saw intense devoted love, and I saw what you are currently calling narcissism. The self. The small (s) self. "The world revolves around me and you need to give me what I want." I saw many levels of mental and emotional disturbance. As I was growing up, this offered me an opportunity to see the two extremes of choices offered here in the earth plane. However, I became mixed up. I became a reflection of both of the opposites. There was what you would think of as a war going on inside me. I could be kind and loving and absolutely filled with joy and, the next moment, I could crawl into my cave, pull the rock in behind me and not care if the world disappeared. In fact, at those times, I wished that it would disappear or I would. This led to trying to disappear. There were moments when I tried to numb myself either with the alcohol or with the drugs. I simply did not feel as if I could take any more. THERE ARE SO MANY CHILDREN FEELING THIS WAY RIGHT NOW.

There are several reasons. One is of course the acceleration of the earth plane; all energy is vibrating at a much faster *frequency and continues to do so. The second is the fact that the status quo in the earth plane, the thinking and the feeling are in complete flux. We are in the time where we are trying to do a one-eighty. We go very strongly in the direction of: "If you can control the physical and the material, you can control your LIFE. If you can prove control over the material, you will be HAPPY."*

Well, we have proven this is not true. So now, in the last four generations, there has been a significant shift in the knowing that this is not true, and those who come in now, in the teen years, are coming in at the height of the flux. Because of this, we add this to what you think of as teen angst anyway. As you know, entering what you know as the teenage years is when we begin to develop a sense of knowing there is a difference between me and I, you out there and something in the great unknown. This can be a very confusing time.

Then we add the urges of the physical body, and a society that says, "Don't you dare follow those urges! They are dirty; they are nasty!" Therefore we think, "Okay, I'm dirty and I'm nasty. Well who am I, what am I?" So we add these together and we see what is happening to our teenage population.

Now we add the third thing. It has become acceptable in many societal groups to use chemicals to deaden the senses. Numb the pain. It has become more and more acceptable to use pharmaceuticals of all kinds, especially in our western nations. The acceptability of using them illegally has also increased.

We have these three issues combining to create a sense of confusion within the population, and it is much more intense than it used to be. It is so much easier now to get whatever you need to shift your mood and numb the senses. And it's OK, it's fun. This is the belief.

Add that to the fact that we are in complete flux and in the teenage years, what you will get is helpless, hopeless confusion. When I was in the "down periods," I was very fortunate. I did see the devotion. There was someone in my life who believed in "Divine Love," who believed in unconditional love, devotion and service. For that reason, I was able to bring myself back out. Whenever I went into the cave, I would either be yanked, kicking and screaming out of the cave, or I would come out willingly because of what I knew, because of what I had seen. The examples of love. That is why many people saw me as two opposites. They knew I could be very creative, very happy, very, very loving. And yet those who were close to me also saw the other side of me who went into a cave and just wanted to be left alone.

Now, I would also like to speak about the grief I felt within my physical body. I did not know what the grieving was for. I realized soon after I crossed over that the grief was a MISSING OF THE PERFECTION OF LOVE.

Another thing that is happening now on the earth plane is that the veil between this side and the other has become much thinner and it continues to become much thinner. As we children in these last few generations are growing up, there is still a societal conditioning that says, "The physical is all there is, so you better be good at the material. That's where your success is; that's what's going to bring you happiness." Yet these generations of children come in with a much closer remembering of Divine Love. A remembering of what we truly are with each other. The fact is, we truly are ONE. That we flow together in harmony, and so the confusion is increased because we do have that memory. I realized that the grief that passed through my body, mind and emotions was a longing for that which I knew was missing; I just didn't know what it was. And so I numbed myself. Sometimes I was able to lose myself in music, but even then, the sorrow and the grief would come through. So I would say to those of you who have children, "Look for that yearning within the child, for that is the soul yearning. They are remembering something at the emotional level that those in the older generations did not bring in with them."

But now, now it is time. It has been for five or six generations that individuals have come with a much clearer idea of the truth of how we feel. So when your children become confused and begin to numb themselves to control their emotions, assist them in finding out who they are. This is the question they want answered. However, most of them believe the question they want answered is: "How can I get something that will make me happy? Why am I so confused?"

If you can help them understand where their power comes from, THEY WILL NOT CHOOSE THE EXIT I DID. We do not mean to say, "You must worship. You must call it God; you must call them angels and Masters." No, it is simply finding out the greater truth of life. Truth is highly personalized. Very, very subjective. And so the wise parent will give the child opportunities for information, encourage them, speak with them, even debate with them, but allow them to find their own truth. Bring them to the help they need.

Now, we would speak about the epidemic of the drug issue that is so prevalent now in the United States. This is in keeping with the training that has been in place in society for over one hundred years that says, "If you do not feel good, it's not good to not feel good, TAKE A PILL, AND THAT WAY YOU CAN CONTINUE TO FUNCTION." That way you will feel good. For the belief has not been: "Oh, this is a sign of trouble; we need to find the cause." Rather, it has been: "That is the trouble. That is the cause, so let us simply cover the pain and the cause is gone."

Now we are beginning to know better. This is not to say pharmaceuticals are bad, for they are not. It is as anything in the earth plane; they are not good or bad, depending on how you use them, and what you use them for. What we are talking about is using pharmaceuticals to escape the purpose. Whether that purpose is a hurt foot telling you that you are not moving forward in the right direction or a grieving heart telling you that you need to find out what else there is in life.

One of the reasons I crossed as I did was to scare the heck out of my friends. Some of it has worked. We made the agreement on the other side, before my leave-taking, of who would be directly involved, based partly on who was most at risk for doing the same thing I did, or worse. And some because they were strong enough to help the others. It is a high risk for a very high gain. We would answer any questions that have come up.

Regina: John, one of the struggles I have was that two of your friends were sent to somewhat of a lockdown facility and they lived. These are not the highest vibrating places on earth. You, of course, did not live, and so it would seem as though I did the wrong thing. I know there are both extremes, one where I allowed you to ease your pain through alcohol and pot. I became very upset when I knew there was the use of pills because I felt this was a real danger, once the pills got involved. What message would you have for parents about whether or not to put a child who is already struggling with this into one of those places?

John: If there is a sign of responsibility for self, then you question whether or not you put them in a lockdown facility. The second thing you look for is desire to heal. Now, these two of whom you spoke had the desire to heal but it had become very, very weak. The willingness to do whatever it took to heal was no longer there, as was seen by the individuals around them. They were going down hill fast. Do not condemn the choice that was made for these two because it is very probable that's what allowed them to stay here and continue to work through. They were losing the battle. Even though the desire was there, it was no longer strong enough to combat the temptation, the habit and the availability. One of the issues that kids deal with is the fact that EVERBODY DOES IT. When you feel alone anyway, to then be told you can no longer be with the friends, the only people you call friends because they do the drugs is sometimes more than the individual child can take, and much more than they are willing to give up. The difference with me was there was still hope. I did still want to heal; I did still keep coming up. With my friends, they weren't coming up any more.

Regina: Then these are the signs parents need to look for.

John: Yes, the two main criteria are responsibility and desire, and you must remember it is not just words; it must be actions and consistent behavior. If the behavior making the changes is not consistent, it is not going to produce anything. So first you look at the responsibility, then you look at the desire, the intensity of the desire.

Regina: Your desire was there at the end, wasn't it, sweetie?

John: Yes. Yes and it resurfaced frequently enough to make itself known, to become stronger than the temptation. Could you have put me in a lockdown facility? Might I still be here? It's possible. We all know that we create our future through God's will so it is possible. But the decision was made in this manner specifically to bring through the information.

Regina: Las Vegans have a 350% higher chance of dying of a drug overdose than the national average. Is there something you can tell me to do to help turn that around?

John: It is time for the quiet majority to become un-quiet. Now, part of the issue you deal with in Las Vegas is the fact that it is built on material desire. It is built on the desperate hope of dreams coming true through the physical. That is a lack of self-responsibility. It is searching for Divine Providence through a means that is anything but Divine. It is also so very easy here because there are certain elements that control this city that are directly tied in with the financial aspect of the drugs. Until the quiet majority makes things too uncomfortable for this to continue, it will continue.

Regina: Am I a part of arousing the quiet majority?

John: Yes. There are many people on many different levels who are becoming the aroused, the no longer quiet majority. The mother who will stand up to the principal and stomp her foot and say, "NO, this is not acceptable." The one who will write a book about the death of her son, and the one who will look at the child and say, "No, this is not your friends' fault; you are the one who decided to do it. You will take responsibility for these consequences." They are all members of the no longer quiet majority. And it begins to move. It is a slow wave at the moment. Still, money holds its sway. That is considered the lifeblood of this city. It is also tied in directly with the current educational system and the economic system. The current educational system is not supported by the economy and therefore there is a strain upon those who would teach the children well. Even those who love the children dearly and come into this profession of teaching with passion are not allowed to teach what needs to be taught. Or they simply have so much to do they cannot touch the children individually in the heart. A part of the change we are now beginning to feel is the entire educational system shuttering. Imagine you have built a two-hundred-story building and it's facing the wrong direction. We need to turn it around. This is beginning to happen.

Now, bottom line. When the attitude is that recreational drugs are not tolerated and not acceptable by more than fifty percent of the population, and they will speak up about this, then we will see a massive shift. The biggest crackdown on what you call the drug trafficking will start in the small pockets, small communities, the parent/teacher associations. It will grow.

Regina: Is there a direct relationship between the use of Ritalin and the subsequent use of cocaine?

John: We would say it is rather an indirect relationship. What is happening is the children are becoming accustomed to having their moods adjusted artificially. Again, we put the band-aid on the cancer. The pain is the problem; the pain is the cause so let us cover up the pain rather than getting to the actual cause and changing it so there is no more pain. What we are doing is creating chemical, emotional dependency on pharmaceuticals because we have not yet acknowledged the better way. We have it, but we have not yet acknowledged it. There is a component in Ritalin that would give a matched frequency to the harsher drug but there are many children on Ritalin who will never take the harsher drug.

Regina: Good. As for the sound from the tuning forks running through the rose quartz crystal for use in Emotional Freedom Techniques, does that have the effect I was looking for? Are the effects exponential because of the combination of sound and light in releasing negative emotions?

John: Yes. If you will remember, quartz itself is a clarifier, and so what happens is a fine-tuning of the vibrational frequencies. That fine-tuning takes place in the quartz as the filter. It also helps the vibrational frequency in strength. Imagine the difference in the ripples in the water if you throw a pebble in the water or if you throw a boulder in the water. The quartz creates the ripples more like the boulder. Remember, this is a pioneering effort. Vibrational frequency healing is in its infancy. You are just beginning to understand what is happening. Think of what is happening in vibrational healing as the same as medical science in the seventeen hundreds. One of the key purposes of this light and sound healing is to shake us up. It is to get us to look at other possibilities. It is to make us uncomfortable in what we think we know, because it is so very different.

Regina: Do you have any advice for me?

John: We would give advice to you and to anyone involved with this project in anyway. REMEMBER, EACH CHILD IS A VERY, VERY UNIQUE EXPRESSION OF DIVINE SPIRIT, and you cannot pigeonhole them according to what anyone else has done. It is important to keep the light of the uniqueness alive in each child, for that is the essence of spirit they are bringing in more brightly than those of the older generations. It is not an easy time to be a parent because we have both of the opposites fully active right now. When we have both of the opposites fully active, it is a constant balancing act. We would, however, say to EVERY parent: "Do not be afraid to do the right thing. Do not to be afraid to stand by your principles. Don't be afraid your child is not going to like you. You are the parent; that is the role you play. Sometimes as a parent, you see your children making wrong choices, choosing things that are going to hurt them, and you know this. If they decide they are going to hate you for the rest of their lives, at least they have the rest of their lives. They will have more time to work it out. And we assure you, they will not hate you for the rest of their lives. DO NOT LET THE CONFLICT FRIGHTEN YOU! When light comes into the dark, there does not have to be conflict, but if there is resistance, there will be. Since that is how we have set it up here at the moment, that's OK. Do not be afraid to wear the warrior guise.

In closing, always, always, always remember Divine Purpose. Divine Purpose is that we return to harmony. That we bring to this earth plane the Joy of the heavens. It says in one of your favorite prayers, "on earth as it is in heaven." What that means is, we have made the agreement that we will bring the joy and beauty and light of the heavens and recreate it exactly the same way in the earth. AND SO WE SHALL. If not today, then tomorrow.

Afterword

At he end of this channel, it felt to me that the "others" spoke with John. What I mean by that is, the other spirits who came in for the channel from the higher realms joined as one voice. Such wisdom and truth resonated with those words. I have friends who are Reborn Christians and I am sure the words would ring true if a pastor spoke them but, since they are channeled from my son who died of a drug overdose or channeled by anyone for that matter, they would be considered evil. As was mentioned in the channel, these beliefs are very personal.

As he spoke the words: "DO NOT LET THE CONFLICT FRIGHTEN YOU," I realized conflict always frightens me. I do not know if my fear of conflict would have stopped me from saving John's life if the only way would have been to piss him off with any type of intervention. I used to tell him I would never bail him out of jail but I feel certain I would have. I would have hoped the lesson would have been learned by just going to jail overnight. I see so many mothers who try to get their children arrested to save their lives and I respect them. I think those of us who listen to our hearts ultimately know what our children need in each circumstance. Each day, their needs are different and each circumstance must be taken into consideration. It is my hope that these words in this book help just one person. That is my fondest wish for then, I will have done my job. Yaya Con Dios.

Statistics 2004: Death by Overdose

As I began to research the number of accidental deaths due to overdoses in this country I was shocked and horrified. The total population of the United States is 303,109,527 and the population of Clark County, Nevada is 1,777,539 (or about 0.6% of the total US population). The total deaths by accidental overdose were 19,838 in the US and 401 in Clark County, Nevada, which is 2.0% of the US total deaths). So, in Clark County, the rate of death by overdose rate is 350% higher than the national average.[1]

Aside from the overwhelming numbers, two things were totally unexpected. The first was that Las Vegans have a 350% higher overdose rate than the national average. The second was that the victims are not only teenagers and young adults. I was amazed to see the problem in all age brackets, including many senior citizens. These numbers horrified us, and worse, the numbers are increasing annually. (I remember feeling the same way when I first read how willingly the Jews walked into the gas chambers in WWII.) We may as well put handguns and grenades into our medicine cabinets for our families to play with.

I have always felt I was my son's first drug pusher for putting him on so many drugs before the age of seven. I feel guilty for looking the other way when it came to beer and pot but the truth is, most of us self-medicate and are all brainwashed into thinking we need a pill to solve all of our problems. It wouldn't surprise me if Americans line up for a pill that whitens your teeth with a list of side effects a mile long. I am not advocating to stay away from all medications but most of the prescriptions Americans take are either supposedly preventative or are for things that could be handled with some self-responsibility in diet, exercise or nutrition, not to mention Vibrational Medicine.

---

1   From the Clark County Coroners office or found on the Internet.

References

Emotional Tapping Techniques: The Journey

If you are interested in the journey of self-healing for you or your family, the field of Energy Psychology is the place to start. This is a trademarked modality by Paul Gallo, the author and expert in the field. The more you use these modalities, the more you realize the power you have to change your thoughts and beliefs consciously. If affirmations and positive thinking alone worked, there would be no need for this entire field. The subconscious plays a huge roll in the Law of Attraction, and Energy Psychology is a map into the subconscious mind. These techniques may seem too simple to work and that is the biggest problem to overcome. We have become used to hard, complicated or chemical solutions to our problems. Until recently, effective ways to process emotions and get rid of deep-rooted belief systems were unknown but just as you would not keep sour milk in your refrigerator, sour emotions and outdated belief systems should be poured out as well.

The place to start is the website of Paul Gallo's at www.energypsych.com.

Another website that is user friendly in Emotional Freedom Techniques (EFT) is designed and maintained by Gary Craig at www.emofree.com, This man has changed the world through his dedication to educating the world about every form of meridian-based tapping techniques. He has the profound ability to stay open to whatever works in the field and encourages all who use this healing modality to contribute their findings to his site. He offers a free, easy to use downloadable 80-page manual, articles by practitioners, and a wonderful newsletter. Ways to use these techniques are astoundingly easy and even more effective.

One of the best books I have ever read on the subject, and there are far too many wonderful books to mention, is *Emotional Self Management* by George Pratt, PhD. and Peter Lambrou, PhD. This book addresses the subconscious belief systems more than most other books. I have trained under these individuals at the classes they give at Scripps Hospital in La Jolla, California.

Another fabulous website that explains in great detail the spiritual components to this work is www.the-tree-of-life.com. Dr. Kurt Ebert has created the CDs that convert sound to a wave that can actually take the place of tapping. I have had the most amazing results with my clients and family.

For adding sound to your healing go to: www.acutonics.com or www.healingsounds.com.

For the basics on salt necessary to hydrate and mineralize your physical body, go to: www.americanbleugreen.com

The Himalayan Crystal Salt and the Stirwands help oxygenate and polarize the body with the least amount of effort and expense. www.hydration101.com is the place to start to raise the vibration of the water you drink and bathe in. The most extensive research is available on this site. Contact Judy Greenough (702) 247-8590.

Another place to learn to raise the vibration and hydration levels of water is: www.jupiterionizers.com and www.enagic.com

For videos and instructional articles by Regina Murphy go to: www.loveinactioninc.com

For the channeled jewelry by Susan Goecke, go to: www.AngelicallyGuided.com

For information on Dr. Fabian, go to: http://web1.greatbasin.net/~sprang/index.php.

To contact Rev. Cheryl J. Johnson, M. Msc., Ht. Masters of Metaphysical Science, Certified Hypnotherapist, Metaphysical Minister, Channel, Dream Interpreter, go to website www.cherlyjjohnson.com, email cheryl@cheryljjohnson.com or call (702) 558-6889

To contact Cattel, Certified Hypnotherapist, Astrologer, Psychic and Media Personality, Channeler and Spiritualist Minister, go to: www.Cattels.com or email cattelcattel@hotmail.com or call (702) 796-0006

For Michele Avanti, CAP, one of less than fifty astrologers worldwide accredited in fixed star astrology (Reno, Nevada) call: (775) 673-6568

To view a shocking one-minute video about death by overdose, a documentary made about my son that has helped many, go to www.youtube.com and type in the words "What Oxycontin Can Do For You."

End Note

It is no wonder John always had a guitar, mandolin or a ukulele in his hand and had to play one of them before he left the house. He even kept his ukulele at work to play before going on an errand. I know it was difficult for him to leave his home environment. He was self-medicating by sending sound directly into his body from the vibration of the strings. Sound on those meridian points at the end of the fingertips helped a great deal.

I would like to address my doubts about the prediction of his early passing and if I could have kept him here in physical form if I had done things differently. Even with all the information in this book and all John has said to me, both in formal channelings and with my close connection to him, there will always be that tiny doubt that I did the wrong thing. My heart knows the truth but my mind still questions. That is the part of us that makes us human and I am grateful to play the game.

Appendix A

Mother Mary Channel by Samara at the Heavenly House (September 2005)

First of all thank you for coming

Whether or not you see me in the window tonight is a chance to do a number of things I believe it is time to do. First and foremost, for each of you hopefully to know, I mean to really know, who you are. To set aside any sense that you are, in any way, not absolutely magnificent. All of your life up until now, whoever might have said, or whatever might have led you to believe, that you are in any way less than magnificent, I implore you to kiss it goodbye. Let's do it everybody. Whatever it was, whatever happened, say goodbye because it really can be that simple. It really can be.

What we really are asking of you and appearing everywhere; movie theaters, office buildings, pieces of bread, everywhere – is to let you know you are the miracle. The miracle is not the window. The miracle is that your energy and your love transform the physical world. Let me say that again. The miracle is that your energy and your love is what transform the physical world. For in that moment, and more and more moments, what I call grace comes and lives with you. For grace is when you and love join, and express your beautiful, beautiful self.

So, in a world still locked in duality, in drama, in tragedy, in difficulty and in all sorts of things one could drown in, we need all of the strong swimmers that you are. It is not that the world is wrong; they simply haven't learned how to swim. And what do I mean by that? If you think about swimming, you throw yourself into a body of water, whether it's a swimming pool, a lake or an ocean, and if you don't move and you don't know how to float quite, you sink, right? And so by learning the laws of gravity and the laws of energy of your body, you can transform that experience from drowning to enjoying your swimming in water.

Those of you who have studied astrology know this is the year that water is being offered for transforming. But to be a strong swimmer, know you each have the capacity to take your own energy and be in your life in a way that you are the one creating the dance, the movement and where you want to swim rather than drown. In your lives, you each know people who are in various stages of drowning. And so how do we teach them to swim? That's where you come in. That's where you each come in. Because first of all, you have to learn how to swim. Because if you don't swim and they don't swim, it's NOT a good outcome. So to swim is really to learn how you can be in your life in a way that is graceful, beautiful, positive, loving and strong. How do you do that? We will talk about some ways in just a moment.

Once you learn that (the children know it all the time), I wish you would teach all of us better, because you learn in any given day: WHEN I AM PRESENT, I'm a strong swimmer. When I am present. I've been telling people for a long while now, YOUR PRESENCE IS YOUR PRESENT. There is a lot in those words. Your PRESENCE, how you show up in your life, in your world, is your gift, you're present to the world. It is also your present reality, as opposed to the past or the future.

It is your present, and so when you are in the precious present, you are a strong swimmer, and therefore you are able to give help to those who otherwise might not make it through whatever difficulty they are experiencing. And beyond that, you can share with them how to become a strong swimmer.

In today's world how do you offer this? How do you teach people to become strong swimmers? Well, there are all kinds of wonderful modalities. Many of you have learned all forms of Energy Medicine, and new things that are just beautiful. New things based on old things that are wonderful. Learning about your body and the energies you carry, and how to bring those energies out into the world in beautiful ways to become strong swimmers.

Becoming a strong swimmer requires that you know about the currents and the wind, and about any obstructions and obstacles that would be in your path as you are swimming so you can negotiate in a world that continues to allow you to feel your preciousness, to feel your beauty, to feel how powerful you are.

So I came to tell you that this coming year 2006 is a very good time to be a good swimmer. And what does that mean? Consider, for instance, the people right now who had to leave New Orleans and leave everything. Imagine, one day you have a car; a house and everything that goes with it, and the next day you have nothing. The beautiful thing is, as they come to the new cities, those cities in general have said, "How can we help you? How can we help you learn to swim again? How can we help you with housing and jobs and all that you require?" What's going on is that your ability to teach people and find out what they require, and to offer it to them, are what has shifted in this year 2005. As you move into 2006, you are going to be given opportunities to really get how much you can change the world. WOW! Sounds pretty big. Well how do you change the world? One moment at a time, one breath at a time, one smile at a time, one act of kindness or love at a time. And that sounds so, "Oh, well yes, I know that," but take just a moment and look back on these past few days. Recently it was the fourth anniversary of September 11. Did you feel any act of kindness coming to you and did you offer any act of kindness, let's say in the last week, anyone?

(YES from Gina) Could you share what happened?

"I work for the fire department and we have sixty-three individuals deployed to New Orleans, and I helped a couple of women who were having road blocks to get over those road blocks. And we put together the beginning of a family support group for those people who are deployed, and it all came together just perfectly."

I really want you to feel the energy of that and join with her to feel the energy of that. And there were obstacles, but you see, that's part of becoming a good swimmer. You don't say, "Oh well, I can't do it," or, "It hasn't been done," or, "Mother said I shouldn't," or whatever. Instead, you ask, "How do we do it? How do we do it?"

When you address it in that way, the situation allows for the force of your love to move through or around those obstacles and create something new. What you've just done has not really ever been done the way you've just done it. I am so appreciative that you shared that experience, because when you begin to see those acts of kindness and love in a sense, energetically, like beautiful rainbows or circles of light, you are beginning to see each connection that was made with the light. Now how does someone feel when someone else is kind to them? Naturally, they are going to offer that kindness back through the next person who comes into their life. And so you do change the world in that way. And part of what has come about since September 11 is that all over the world, people begin to see that life is somewhat fragile. If we are not helping each other, if we are not reaching out to each other, we really are missing the boat. And yet some of the past inertia has been, "Oh well, you know, I really shouldn't get involved."

The new opportunity is to realize: If not now, when? If not me, who? So into your lives every day are coming those opportunities. And even if you feel, in your mind, that you don't know what to do, your intention and your willingness to put yourself in the water, to say, "Well, I know they need food, support, love, housing, so let me see what I can do. Let me volunteer; let me go talk to someone." NOW it starts to shift. There are so many ways to talk about this but I will simply use an analogy. And if I mix my metaphors, please forgive me. What is really going on here is the birth of Heaven? Bringing heaven here. What is heaven but a place of love? And so what's going on is that the energetic patterns that have served the Earth but have kept things in the status quo for a long time are now being shaken, burned, drowned, you name it, so that a new energy can be created here. Out of the chaos, out of these difficulties, out of this suffering, you come, you stand, you swim, and you reach out your hand, you love and the world changes.

So it is absolutely time in which you are being given these opportunities to really live from your highest self, from your deepest heart, from your greatest love ... and it's a very exciting time. In that sense, there are so many new things to be created that haven't yet been here for the family of man. There are new forms of education, of healthcare, of food, of communication, of housing – all sorts of things just waiting to come through you. And again, you don't have to say, "Well I don't know what to do, or how to do it." Just say YES to your greater spirit and it shall be done.

It's really about understanding that maybe you had a difficult experience in the past doing this or doing that. And so, a part of your being says, "Well, when I did that a couple of years ago, it didn't work out very well." It's realizing that maybe so, it didn't work out a couple of years ago, but the time is different now. You are different now. And when you allow your self to be really aligned with your divine template, your heaven arrives. Your heavenly experience for you, and therefore for what you are going to offer into the world. And now, all over this country especially, people are realizing they have the ability to give food and housing and resources to the thousands of people who left New Orleans.

Now if you think for a moment: "Where is that food? Where is that blanket? Is it still in the attic or garage or basement?" So what's happening is that the energy is being freed up, along with the attitude or mentality of, "I have to protect what's mine. That box of food IS MINE." That too is over, and it never really belonged to you anyway. You might have been caring for it, and we appreciate that, but none of it ever belonged to anyone.

So when you start to understand that, as you allow your energy to be aligned with your divine purpose, you allow the energy to flow to you, through you and out in whatever way you are guided to do. So you always have enough! You'll always have enough. You will always have what you are to have. And you're always creating, because you're sharing that energy in a beautiful flow.

What happens when energy is stopped? It becomes stagnant. If you look at it from the economic point of view, there certainly was tremendous devastation in New Orleans, but now when people start giving back to these lovely souls who have chosen to go through this experience, they are starting new lives. They are putting their energy into the different cities they relocated to.

So I encourage all of you, tonight, tomorrow and the next day, to look around your houses. If you have things stuffed in drawers, in boxes, in attics and basements that you haven't even looked at for ten years, consider that it's not serving you. And perhaps by freeing yourself of them, new things can come to you. So the world is trying to balance itself.

There is enough food for everyone, enough shelter for everyone, enough work for everyone, enough money for everyone. But, what is required is an understanding that you are here to share your love and your energy. And it's certainly absolutely fine to be in a beautiful place and to have beautiful things. I'm speaking of the things stuffed in closets and basements or attics that you don't even see or use. As those storehouses are freed, equality in the world rebalances.

Of those who, because of strife and anger, have struck out at America and other countries, why did they do this? In many cases, it was because of years and years of subjugation. And when people are in subjugation, their spirit wants to be free. And they are also feeling, "Someone must be to blame for my subjugation." And so whatever propaganda has been in their life leads them to choose their enemy and they strike out at that enemy. But imagine if everyone in the world had enough to eat, had safety in their lives, a roof over their head for themselves and their family, how interested would they be in blowing up your country?

So understand that you will have the world that you create. If you are sending out love, energy, kindness, blankets and whatever else you can, what is coming back to you is love, kindness and energy to buy more blankets, or whatever you want in your life. So, it's a beautiful time for that.

None of you would be here tonight unless this was the conversation you needed to hear tonight. This is a beautiful truth to come in 2006, when the world can begin to see that kindness is a commodity. Sometimes if you give only money, it's not enough. Because if only money is given, sometimes the person still feels powerless. But in the kindness of the money, the blanket, whatever you're giving, there is a sense of "I am ONE with YOU. We live on this Earth together, and in this moment, yes, I'm giving you a blanket, but I'm here with you and there is equality."

That's so important. So this is a year when kindness and compassion along with your generosity can really transform the world in such beautiful ways.

There is one more matrix I want to speak about. The matrix of fear can be very strong. Anyone here ever feel fear? It can be very strong. And so coming out of this is trusting in yourself and your energy and your courage, so the fear of, say, "Will I lose my job?" or, "What can happen if I risk this or that?" must be mitigated by your knowing what is right to do. For this is also a year of what I call the Founding Mothers. The Founding Mothers? Hmm. Remember the Founding Fathers? They did a beautiful job and now it is time to take all of that wisdom of the Founding Fathers and marry it to the Founding Mothers. What that really means is that this land of the free and the home of the brave, as you call it, really does become the land of the free and the home of the brave.

Already you have so many brave people; you see them in every walk of life. But it is also time, just as when the Founding Fathers went against England. Imagine, at that time, it was quite an amazing thing to do, to go against the king. To start a new country, to refuse to be subjugated to that authority which was not of the people, by the people and for the people. Huge! Marvelous! And so I am encouraging all of you to go back to: "Of the people, by the people and for the people." Start to ask, "What does that really mean?"

And so, what you've just done through your fire department by reaching out is really of the people, by the people and for the people. Whatever your allegiance in your government, Democrat, Republican, and Independent Libertarian, whatever understands it is also open to new ideas. They must be spoken, they must be offered, and they must be a part of the conversation. Or else they will not occur.

That is not to bash the government; it is to ask, "What can we do instead that is of the people, by the people, for the people"? And, of course, that is for the entire world, not only for America. But here in America, you have really been given a special opportunity because you have a very young country and a very diverse country. So in a funny way, you have a little less inertia to deal with than those countries that have been established for thousands of years with certain cultural outlooks. And so here, even though there are still laws and rituals that tell you what you should do and not do, there is quite a bit more freedom to move and change to allow for new creations. So it is not any accident that what recently occurred has also stirred other countries to say, "Let us help you."

This has put America in a different position than it is accustomed to, because America is accustomed to helping others. So it is a beautiful time. A beautiful time.

Appendix B

Thought Field Therapy

Dr. Roger Callahan named his modality "Thought Field Therapy" because he believes that when we think about an experience or thought associated with an emotional problem, we tune into a "thought field," the most fundamental concept in the TFT system. Whenever a person thinks about a trauma or emotional problem, he says, encoded information called "perturbations" contained in the thought field become activated. These perturbations are the root cause of negative emotions and each perturbation corresponds to a meridian point on the body. In order to eliminate the emotional upset, Dr. Callahan says a precise sequence of meridian points must be tapped on. Tapping unblocks or balances the flow of chi, or vital life energy.

The sequences for tapping can be determined by two of his proprietary "causal diagnostic" techniques:

1. Muscle testing, or applied kinesiology.
2. Voice Technology, by which Dr. Callahan cures over the phone by analyzing the client's voice. From this, he can determine which points on the body the client should tap.

Dr. Callahan treated his first patient in 1980. She was a 42-year-old woman named Mary, who had a severe lifelong phobia of water that was so bad that she could only take sponge baths. She was even terrified of rain, and could not bear to go near any body of water, especially the ocean. After 18 months of hypnosis, she could sit at the side of a swimming pool, but still felt terrified, with "a horrible feeling in the pit of my stomach."

As an experiment, Dr. Callahan had her tap on the stomach meridian end point, which was under her eye. Immediately, her fear of water vanished and she ran out to the pool, completely unafraid. She could also stand out in rain and walk on the beach with no trace of fear. This was still the case 17 years later.

Dr. Callahan began treating other phobia and trauma patients and, through trial and error, identified various sequences for tapping meridian points. He also developed a procedure called "the nine gamut" – tapping on the back of the hand while performing eye movements, humming, and counting. This is believed to balance the left and right hemispheres of the brain.

A peer-reviewed controlled study by Monica Pignotti on Thought Field Therapy (using Voice Technology) was published in The Scientific Review of Mental Health Practice journal, showed no difference between TFT-VT and random tapping sequences, which suggests that Dr. Callahan's unique proprietary sequences may be unnecessary.

TFT practitioners, however, assert that tens of thousands of clients have been successfully treated with no side effects, and dismiss critics calling the technique "pseudoscience." Because Dr. Callahan imposes sharp restrictions on how TFT Diagnostics are done and taught, several people have modified the modality to come up with their own. The most well known is Gary Craig's Emotional Freedom Techniques, or EFT, in which all the points discovered by Dr. Callahan are tapped over and over. (See Appendix C.)

Appendix C

Emotional Freedom Techniques (EFT)

In the mid-1990s, Gary Craig created EFT as a simplification of and improvement over Dr. Roger Callahan's TFT (see Appendix B). Craig trained with Dr. Callahan in the early 1990s, and was the first person Dr. Callahan trained in Voice Technology. Craig soon discovered that the sequence of tapping points did not matter and that Dr. Callahan's proprietary diagnostics were unnecessary, so he did away with them. In lieu of individual algorithms for specific problems, he came up with a comprehensive "one size fits all" sequence for all problems. This avoids the need for diagnosis or muscle testing.

One EFT practitioner claims, "You can use it for everything from the common cold to cancer." The basic EFT technique involves holding a disturbing emotion or traumatic memory in the mind while simultaneously using the fingers to tap on a series of 12 specific points on the body that correspond to the body's meridians. The principle is that negative emotions are caused by disturbances in the body's energy field and that tapping on the meridians while thinking of a negative emotion changes the body's energy field, bringing it back into balance.

Gary Craig maintains that negative emotions are built in the following stages:

1. Something negative happens to you.
2. As a result, you experience a negative emotion, i.e., you feel bad.

3. The negative emotion leads to negative programming inside the body's energy system, which is disrupted in some way.
4. This disruption influences how you respond to future situations, usually negatively.

EFT removes the negative responses to future situations by eliminating the negative emotion and by restoring the energy field's balance. Most talk therapies stop at dealing with the negative emotions, and can take months or years to work, but EFT goes further by restoring the energy balance, often in two or three sessions. I have found it often to be instantaneous.

So EFT is basically an emotional version of acupuncture without the needles. Instead, you use your fingertips to tap on energy meridian points on the body. Gary Craig's sequence is easy to learn and remember, and you can do it anywhere. The two mantras of EFT are:

- "The cause of all negative emotions is a disruption in the body's energy system."
- "Our unresolved negative emotions are major contributors to most physical pains and diseases."

You can sign up for Gary's newsletter and download a free copy of his EFT manual from www.emofree.com. He emphasizes that the manual is a "starter kit" and that serious practitioners need to study his 5-CD course.

A one-page summary of the technique and the tapping points appears as the last page of this book.

Appendix D

Emotional Sound Technique (EST)

Devised by the author, EST is a modality that combines phrases from Emotional Self-Management, Dr. Callahan/Gary Craig's tapping points, and the use of tuning forks. Instead of tapping on points, I apply specific frequency forks to them and can also run the sound through a rose quartz crystal on the points. I have found the benefits of this to be:

1. It's an effective shortcut to eliminate subconscious sabotage.
2. Immediate release of anger and anxiety.
3. Effective positive results of chosen affirmations.
4. An overall sense of relief of physical and emotional pain.

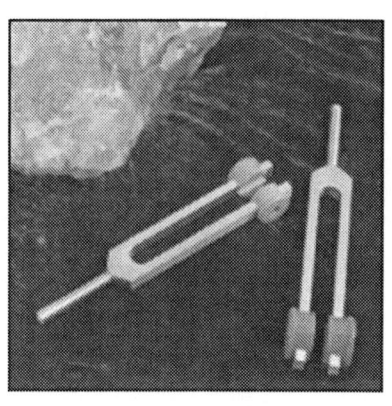

EST is a noninvasive protocol using the OM frequency (136.10 Hz). The fork is applied directly to acupressure points, trigger points, points of pain and charkas to open the energy pathways in the body. Adding the crystal clarifies, filters and amplifies the sound creating a deeper level of healing.

Although great benefit is derived from tapping, a more specific emotional outcome can be achieved by applying a sound that sedates, for instance in cases with trauma, anger or anxiety. A tonifying sound might be used when working with sadness or the desired energy of joy. A more neutral sound might be chosen as a way to gently prepare the body for the other sounds. Sound can affect the receptors on our cells faster than any drug. The crystals have specific vibrations also, making the proper combination very powerful. The basic set for families of an OHM fork and a rose quartz is designed to be safe, simple and very effective for emotional and physical pain. As always more advanced uses are available for training to therapists. The sounds of our own voices are healing tools that we are only now recognizing. EST also incorporates voice into Energy Psychology. This works especially well with children. Information about EST and the "crystal and fork" set can also be found on www.LoveInActionInc.com.

Appendix E

The AIM Program

AIM stands for All Inclusive Method, and the AIM Program provides a method of energetic balancing. The principle is that everything is energy, therefore everything has a frequency. Imbalances such as illness and disease have a unique and characteristic frequency that can be brought into balance and neutralized by applying a balancing energy.

The AIM Program is a spiritual process performed by exposing a participant's photo to subtle-energy balancing frequencies. Because the photograph is part of your spiritual hologram, when your photograph is exposed to these balancing frequencies, you receive these energies, which you can use to help manifest your intention to heal yourself and raise your consciousness. Through their photographs, AIM participants have access to hundreds of thousands of balancing energies 24 hours a day, 7 days a week.

Stephan Lewis, the founder, is quick to point out, "It is important to understand that the AIM Program of Energetic Balancing does not, and cannot, heal you. Only YOU can heal you. Neither EMC² nor AIM diagnose, treat, cure or prevent disease. The AIM Program is a TOOL that YOU can use to heal yourself. Every AIM participant is unique and every participant's experience on the AIM Program is unique."

You can learn more about AIM at:

www.energeticmatrix.com.

or call Judy Greenough at: (702) 247-8590

Appendix J

The Tragic Consequences of Drugging Our Children

[Reproduced with permission from http://articles.mercola.com/sites/articles/

The number of prescriptions for psychotropic drugs for children more than doubled between 1995 and 2000. This revealing documentary by Gary Null1 details the devastating consequences of this excessive medicating of our children with mind-altering drugs. The film focuses on children who have been diagnosed with attention deficit hyperactivity disorder

(ADHD), even though evidence to verify such a diagnosis is lacking. Instead, kids are often labeled with ADHD simply for acting like kids: fidgeting, speaking out of turn, not wanting to sit still, and being hyper.

The diagnosis of ADHD is often made based on anecdotal evidence and standardized assessments from parents and teachers, without giving consideration to other potential factors like home life, diet, and environmental toxins. The end result for kids diagnosed with ADHD, as the video shows, is almost always medications.

If you've ever wondered why kids were rarely committing suicide or violent acts in schools when YOU were growing up, this essential video may shed some insight.

Dr. Mercola comments:

I urge you to devote some time to watching *The Drugging of Our Children*. This is a film that everyone with children should see.

Access the video *The Drugging of Our Children* on the above website page.

You may have noticed the back-to-school themed advertisements for ADHD drugs that came out just in time for parents and teachers to begin questioning which students will "need" these medications. This is a carefully timed marketing scheme aimed at selling more of these potent drugs, such as Ritalin, to your children — and the marketing works. Many adolescent psychiatrists report that there is a sharp increase in prescriptions for ADHD drugs when kids start the school year. Some drug companies are even marketing candy-flavored versions of these drugs. It's no wonder that drugs for ADHD bring in about $1 billion in sales every year. It is ironic that children are urged not to take drugs when it comes to the illegal variety, but are readily supplied with mind-altering medications as long as they are FDA-approved. However, health professionals prescribe these drugs without warning parents about the severe and potentially fatal side effects (psychotic symptoms, headaches, insomnia, hallucinations, cardiac arrhythmia). Many of the drugs used to treat ADHD are not only potentially hazardous, but they are unnecessary if your child is treated appropriately.

How to Treat ADHD Naturally

There are plenty of safe, effective alternatives for treating this condition, and some particularly effective methods include:
- Using plenty of animal-based omega-3 fats like krill oil.
- Spending more time in nature.
- Balancing your intake of omega-3 and omega-6 fats (from vegetables oils).
- Avoiding processed foods, especially those containing artificial colors, flavors, and preservatives, which may trigger ADHD symptoms.

- Replacing soft drinks, fruit juices, and pasteurized milk in your diet with pure water.
- Reducing or eliminating grains and sugars from your diet.

For parents out there, I realize that many decide to put their children on a psychotropic drug because they believe it will help them. There can also be extreme pressure to do so, with some public schools even accusing parents of child abuse when they resist giving their kids drugs such as Ritalin.

What you need to know, and spread the word about, is that:

- These drugs are potent (Ritalin is more potent than cocaine) and produce long-term changes in your child's brain
- They cause serious side effects
- ADHD is almost always related to dietary and environmental factors, and can be cured by making the appropriate changes (outlined above)

Another helpful tool is my three-part interview with renowned children's health expert Dr. Lendon Smith on Non-Drug Treatment of ADD/ADHD. Dr. Smith passed away several years ago, but was really one of the pioneer physicians in this area.

Appendix G: Photo Gallery

#1 This is the client prior to the session beginning. I always check if the hydration and mineral balance is good. In this case it wasn't and she drank a solution of ionized water and 26% Himalayan crystal salt.

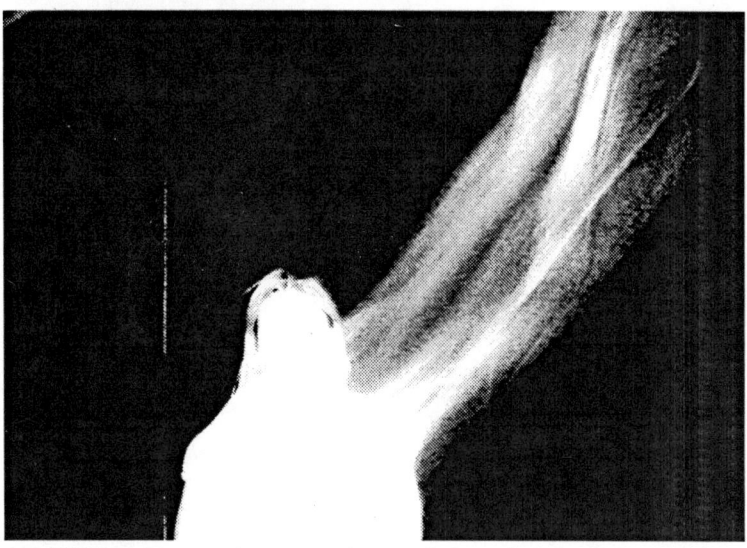

#2 Within minutes, her energy became balanced and stable. According to the book Water and Salt, *it only takes 15 minutes to balance the entire body. It is recommended to drink this solution daily,* a practice begun in the salt hospitals centuries ago. This should not be taken if you have kidney problems or high blood pressure.

#3 My grandson Sam playing my son's guitar the day we gave it to him. The sound is converted to waves in the photo just as Dr. Ebert's Accutone CDs do when the antenna is placed in the boom box.

#4 This woman is tapping on what is called the Psychological Reversal point in Energy Psychology. This is done when a subconscious belief is being released. Sometimes only one side of the brain is affected. In this picture it appears that only the right side of the brain is releasing energy.

#5 Janee Vere singing "Light Language" during a healing session

#6 Janee singing. Her higher self is clear in the photo.

#7 The Tibetan bowls are vibrating during a sacred concert with drums and bowls.

These next five photos (8-12) are of the first session with Susan working with her son Ryan using the rose quartz crystal. The crystal acts as a clarifier and an amplifier.

#8 Susan placed the rose quartz directly on the spot where Ryan's back hurt. She used two forks. The OHM and a frequency that created a perfect fifth, sending a neutral, opening sound into the area. Within two minutes his backache was gone. He said, "It's been hurting real bad for a long time." His back is still fine.

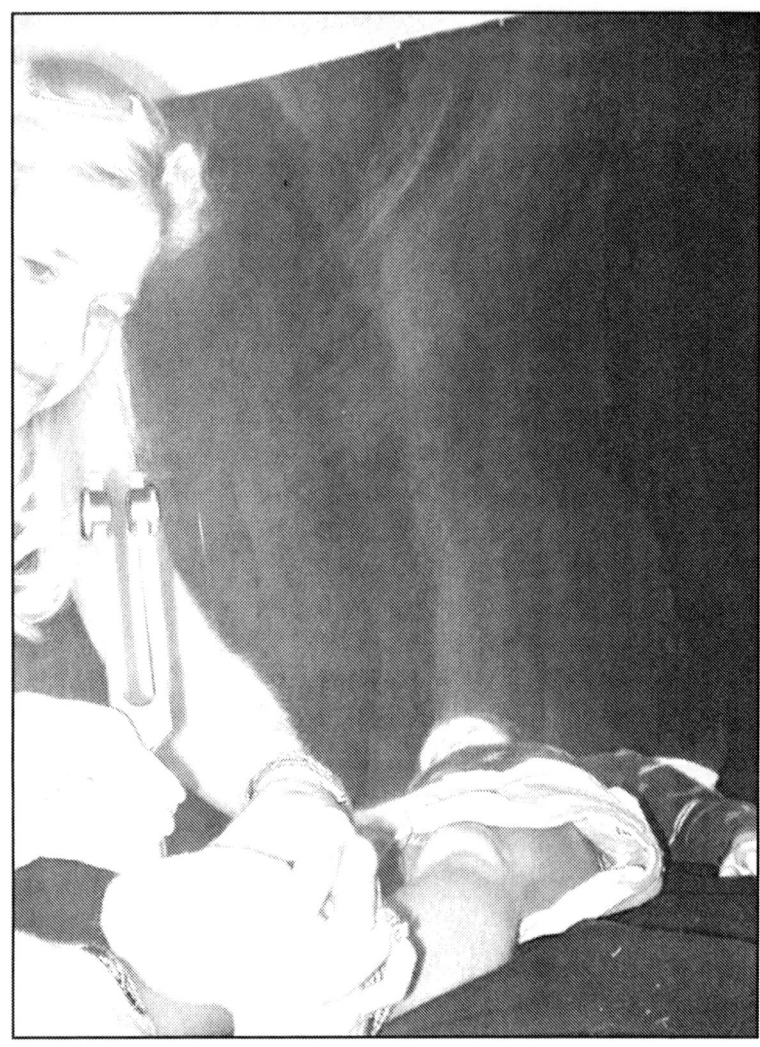

#9 Susan is now working on the anger issue Ryan had at school. The liver four meridian point is being sedated to help release the anger. This is not a typical EFT point. However, it is a major acupressure point for sedating the liver. (The liver holds anger.)

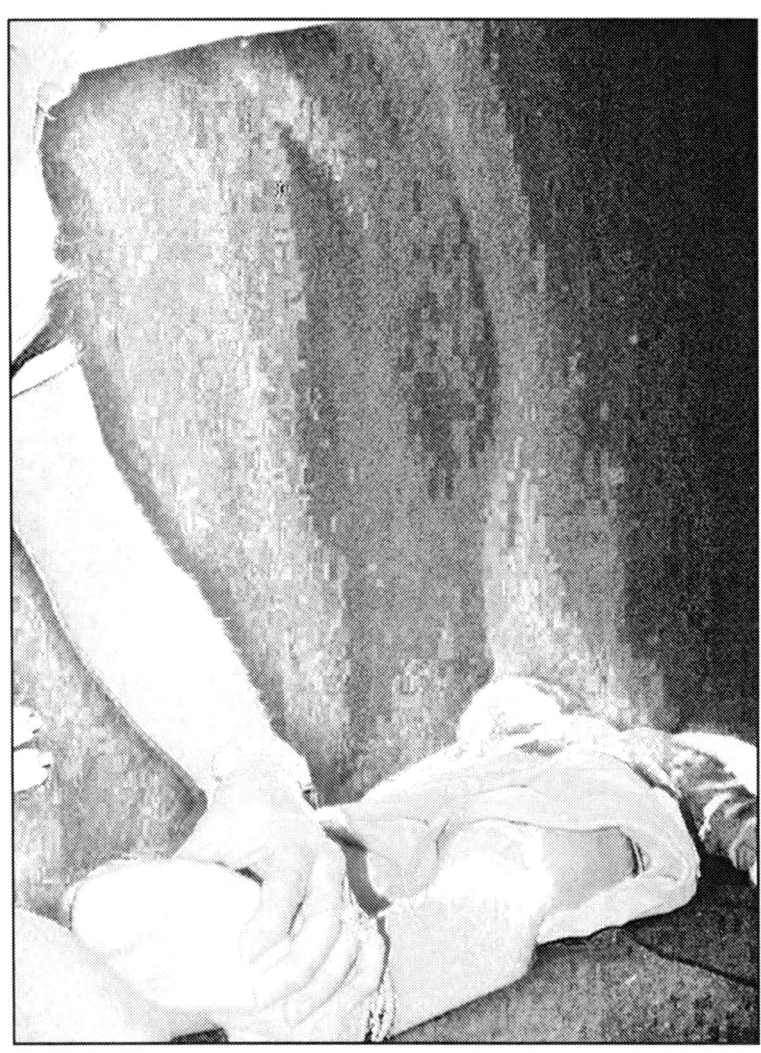

#10 In this photo, more intense energy is being released as she works on that point.

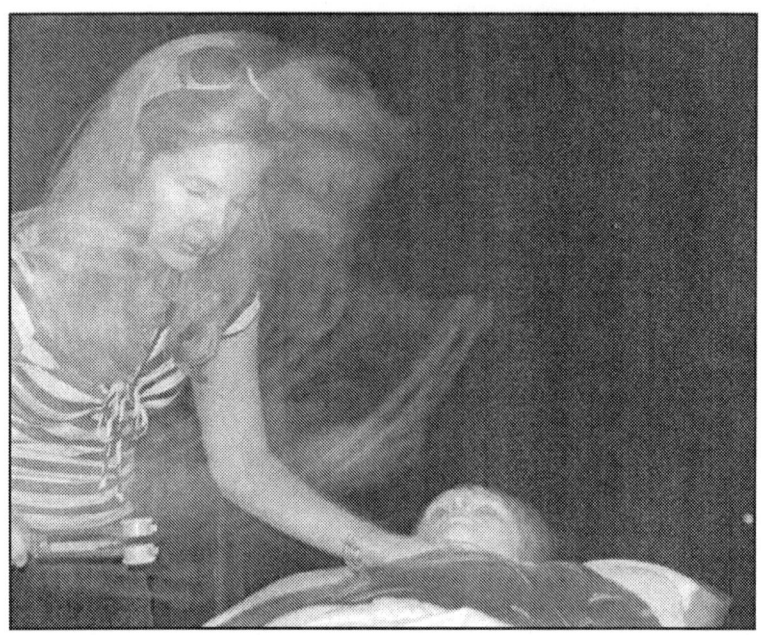

#11 Susan is rubbing the rose quartz crystal on the main Psychological Reversal point while Ryan says, "I deeply and completely love myself even with all this anger." They are still working with the anger.

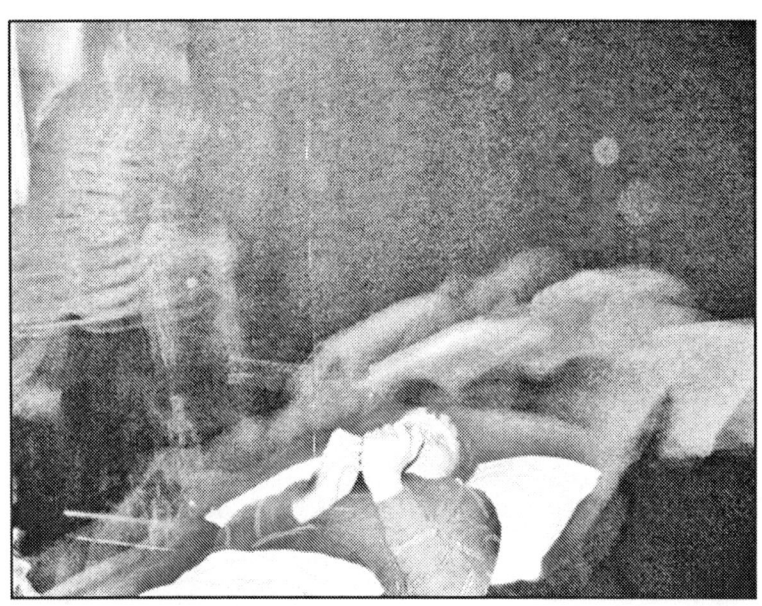

#12 Ryan rubs the rose quartz crystal on the other Psychological Reversal point and continues to say the same thing. Within a few minutes, he cannot feel angry at all when he thinks about what he was upset about.

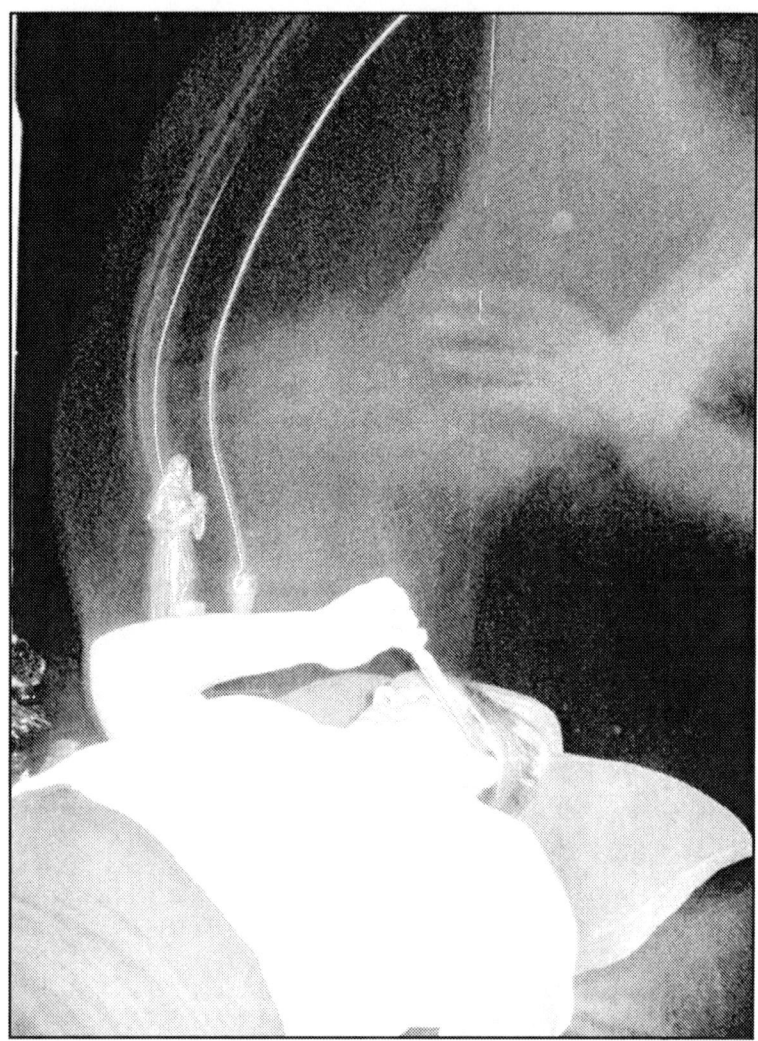

#13 Client as she listens to the "Holy Harmony" forks. These frequencies were found by the sound expert Jonathan Goldman in the Bible and are extremely powerful.

#14 This woman held the rose quartz crystal on her Third Eye and then activated the OHM fork and placed it on the crystal. Her entire auric field is seen here highly activated. She was still glowing the next time I saw her.

#15 This picture is also on the back of the book and shows my sister on our boat and the essence of my son behind her. She just had a stroke and would be facing even more difficult health challenges. After two grueling surgeries she has recovered beautifully.

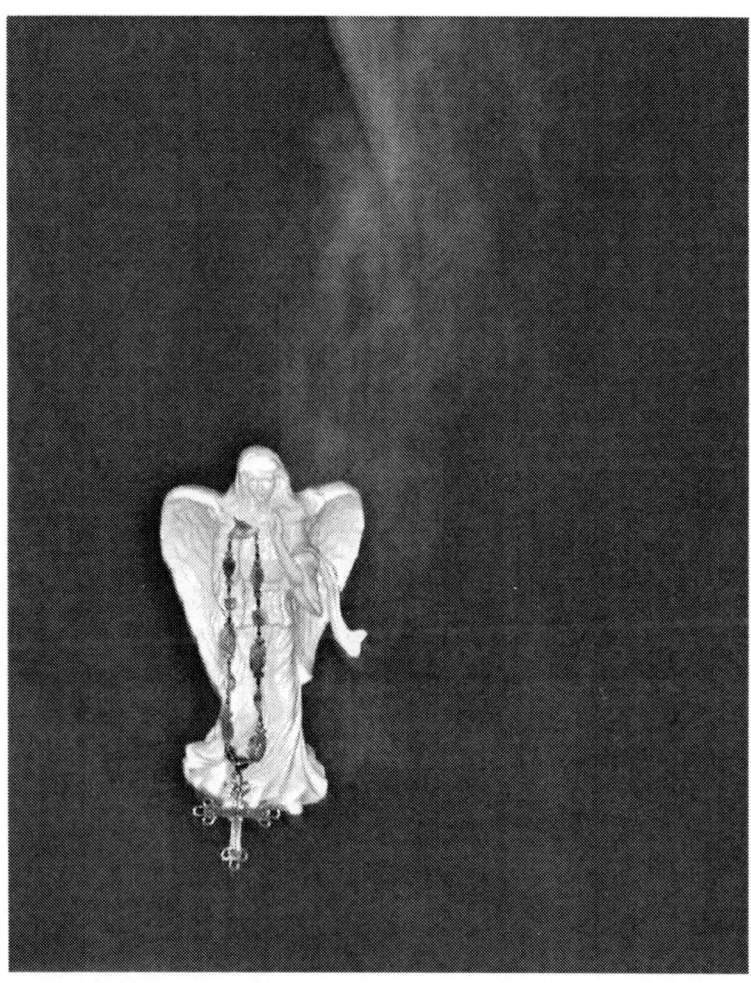

#16 This photo is the original untouched picture of the apparent "Energy of Christ" on the back cover. I was photographing Susan's jewelry. This necklace has a large antique cross on it.

#17 This is the pink light as it shows up in the healing room. I am holding the candle.

#18 My grandson Gino with the pink light on his heart.

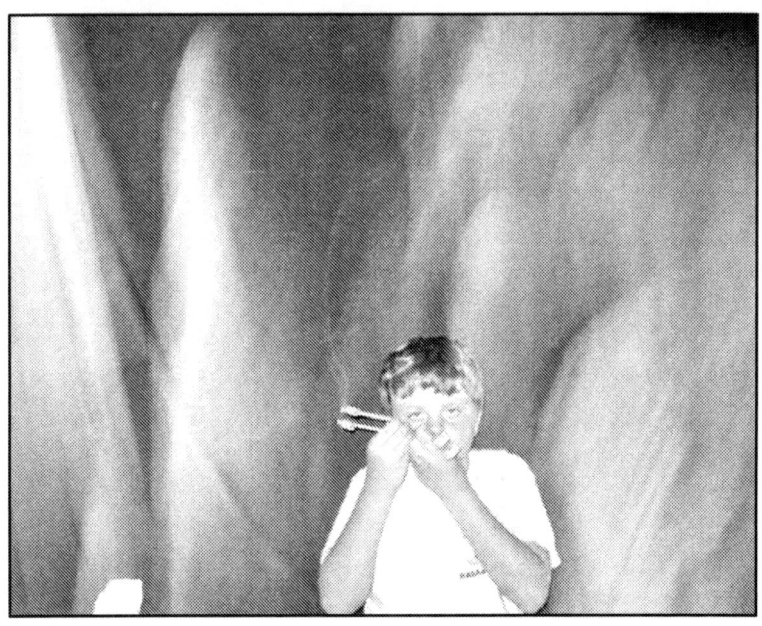

#19 My grandson John as he treats himself with Emotional Sound Techniques (EST). The picture shows streams of energy from the forks as well as his auric field. John is only ten and can treat himself.

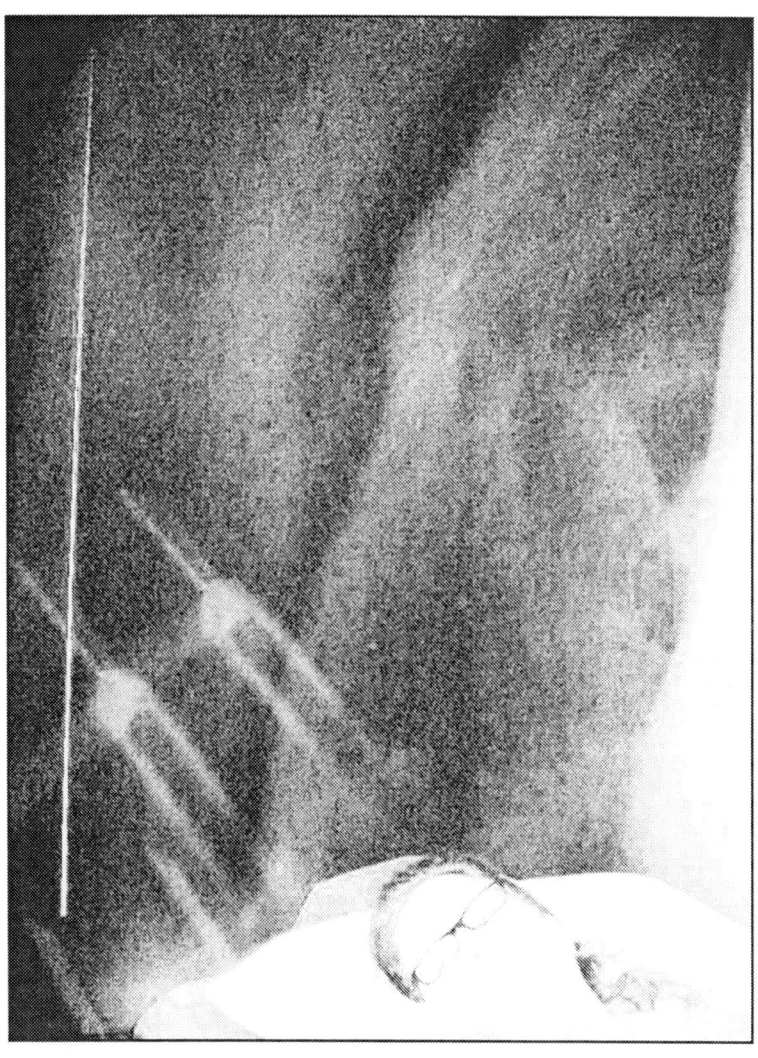

#20 During a session with a hospice nurse, we began discussing what a blessing it would be to use sound to help the souls make their transition to the soul plane.

POWERFUL TAPPING TECHNIQUE
While rubbing on the chest spot (below left shoulder)
(repeat EVERYTHING 3 times)
I deeply and completely accept myself - even with my _____

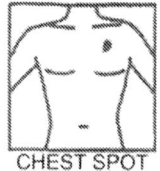

While Tapping on the Brow Spot (EB)
I am healing all the sadness in all the roots and the deepest cause of this problem.

While Tapping Under the Eye (UE)
I am healing all the fear in all the roots and the deepest cause of this problem.

While Tapping on the Little Finger Inside of Nail (LF)
I am healing all the anger in all the roots and the deepest cause of this problem.

While Tapping on the Brow Spot Again
I have healed all the emotional traumas in all the roots and the deepest cause of this problem.

<u>When you feel the problem is gone, you can do the optimizer protocol:</u>
Envision the perfect outcome to the problem you have just worked on and create a positive affirmation. Say the affirmation while Tapping 3 times on each spot: brow (EB), under nose (UN), under lip (LL), and inside nail of middle finger (MF).
<u>Repeat until you believe your statement 100%!</u>

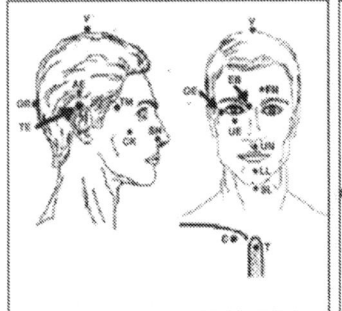
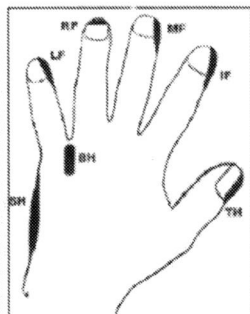

Breinigsville, PA USA
04 March 2010
233592BV00003B/4/A